Wildflowers of
Alabama

AND ADJOINING STATES

Wildflowers of Alabama

AND ADJOINING STATES

Blanche E. Dean/Amy Mason/
Joab L. Thomas

The University of Alabama Press
University, Alabama

CONTENTS

PHYSIOGRAPHIC MAP OF ALABAMA

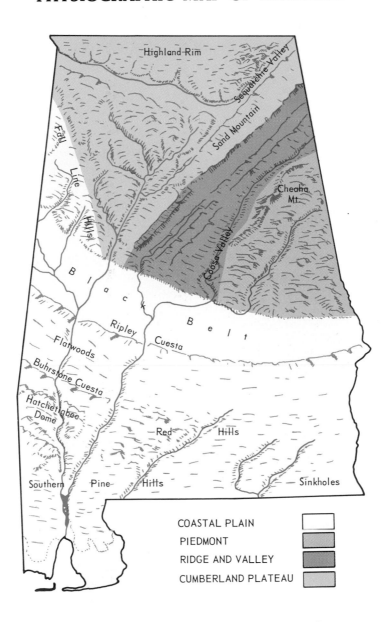

Highland Rim
Sequatchie Valley
Sand Mountain
Fall
Line
Hills
Cheaha Mt.
Black
Belt
Coosa Valley
Ripley
Cuesta
Flatwoods
Buhrstone Cuesta
Hatchetigbee Dome
Red Hills
Southern Pine Hills
Sinkholes

COASTAL PLAIN
PIEDMONT
RIDGE AND VALLEY
CUMBERLAND PLATEAU

From The Atlas of Alabama, Copyright © 1973 by
THE UNIVERSITY OF ALABAMA PRESS.

INTRODUCTION

The rich flora of Alabama, although not yet adequately catalogued, contains almost 3000 species of native or naturalized flowering plants. Few states, indeed, are blessed with a native flora that can compare with the diversity and the beauty of the flowering plants of Alabama. The term *wildflower* is used in a variety of senses, but generally it refers to any flowering plant that occurs outside of cultivation—regardless of whether the species is native or introduced.

With such a wide variety of wildflowers in the state it was difficult to decide which species should be included in a book of this scope. In making these decisions highest priority was given to plants that would be of particular interest to amateur naturalists and wildflower enthusiasts. For this reason special consideration was given to a group such as the orchids whereas a large group such as the grasses is represented by only one species. A few very rare plants, such as the Alabama croton, are included because of their special significance in the flora of Alabama. On the other hand a few very beautiful and very common species were not included because they are so well known that there is scarcely anyone who is not familiar with them.

Although this book treats primarily the herbaceous flowering plants, it also includes a few striking trees and shrubs that have been brought to the authors for identification. The trees and shrubs of Alabama were treated in an earlier work by Blanche Dean—*Trees and Shrubs in the Heart of Dixie.*

Nomenclature

The English or common names and the Latin or scientific names are given for the plant families and for each wildflower illustrated. Many wildflowers have more than one common name—some have more than a half dozen. Because of space limitations, no more than two common names are listed at the beginning of a description, although additional names are included in the index. Common names are inexact, however, and will vary considerably from one part of the country to the next. Moreover, many plants do not have common names, or are lumped together with a group of related species under a single name. For these reasons even amateur botanists are encouraged to use the scientific names whenever accuracy of communication is necessary.

The scientific name consists of three parts—the genus, the species, and the authority. The genus is a group name and consists of one or more related species. For example, *Viola* is the genus or group name for violets. *Viola tricolor* L. is one particular violet, the pansy, or Johnny-jump-up. The initial L. following the name stands for Linnaeus, who first described this species and is thus the authority for the name. In many cases the scientific name will refer to some peculiar characteristic of the plant. Certain ones of particular interest are explained in the description.

In general the sequence and the scientific nomenclature used in this book follow that of the *Manual of the Vascular Flora of the Carolinas* by Radford, Ahles, and Bell, University of North Carolina Press, 1968. This manual is the most recent technical manual published on the flora of the southeastern United States, and it follows the latest International Code of Botanical Nomenclature.

Plant Descriptions

Most of the illustrations are close-up photographs of one or a few flowers. Although the most important characteristics used in the identification of flowering plants are found in the flowers, it is often helpful or even essential to have other information in order to make an accurate identification. This additional information is supplied in the descriptions that accompany the wildflowers illustrated. The descriptions contain primarily information useful in identifying the plant, such as the size and growth habit of the entire plant, the size and shape of the leaves, and the size, color, and any notable variation that might be expected in the flowers. This information is followed by a listing of the months during which the plant usually blooms in Alabama and adjoining states, the habitat in which it is usually found, and the geographic range of the species in the United States. For many species additional information is given, particularly if the plant is poisonous, edible, or has some other special significance.

In describing the habitat of a plant, reference is often made to the major physiographic provinces in Alabama: the Coastal Plain, the Piedmont, the Ridge and Valley, and the Cumberland Plateau. These provinces are shown in the accompanying physiographic map of Alabama. These physiographic references indicate the distribution of the species in Alabama and adjoining states, but not necessarily throughout the range of the species. For example, a species found only in the Plateau region of Alabama may occur in other physiographic provinces farther north.

Flower Structure

Fine details of flower structure are often used to distinguish species and varieties of flowering plants. Thus, it is most important to have a good understanding of the structure of flowers and to be familiar with the kinds of variation in flower structure found in different plant groups.

A typical flower is illustrated in Figure I, page *xvi*, with the different parts labeled. The most common type of flower structure is one consisting of 4 sets of flower parts, usually arranged in cycles. The outermost cycle consists of sepals, and the entire cycle is known as the calyx. Characteristically the sepals are green. The next cycle of parts is composed of petals that collectively make up the corolla. The petals are usually brightly colored and often function to attract insects or other pollinating agents to the flower. The third set of parts consists of one or more cycles of stamens. The stamens are the male reproductive organs of the flower and are composed of a thin filament terminated by an anther, a saclike structure containing pollen. In the center of the flower is the female reproductive structure consisting of one or more pistils. A typical pistil has an inflated basal portion known as an ovary, and an elongate extension above the ovary called the style that is terminated by a structure specialized for catching pollen, known as the stigma.

In certain flowers one or more of these sets of flower parts may be missing, and such a flower is said to be incomplete. Several members of the Buttercup Family, for example, lack petals. In many such cases other parts of the flower, such as the sepals, are modified to resemble the corolla and thus function to attract pollinators. In other flowers that lack petals the flowers may be wind pollinated. These plants usually have small, inconspicuous flowers.

The typical flower structure described above is modified in a number of ways in different plant groups and these modifications often serve as distinguishing characteristics for the groups. These modifications include the fusion of various flower parts, the loss of parts, changes in symmetry, and the clustering of individual flowers into an inflorescence that resembles a single flower. Examples of the more common types of flowers and inflorescences are illustrated in Figure I, page *xvi*. Unusual modifications of flower structure are discussed briefly in the first species description in each family.

Two plant families that have a flower structure that is particularly complex are the Orchid Family and the Sunflower

Family. These families represent the apexes of the two major evolutionary lines of flowering plants, so it is understandable that the flower structure should be complex in these groups. In the Orchid Family the petals are differentiated into two lateral petals that are similar to the sepals and a single, highly modified central or lip petal. The lip petal usually differs in color, shape, and markings from the lateral petals. The stamens and the pistil are fused together, forming a structure known as the column. At the apex of the column there are a stigma and one or two anthers. The shape and structure of the column often provide important characteristics used to distinguish species of orchids.

In the Sunflower Family a number of individual flowers are grouped together into a compact, headlike cluster that resembles a single flower. Two different kinds of flowers have developed in this family and both kinds may be found in the same cluster or flower head. For example, the typical "sunflower" is actually a dense cluster of two different kinds of flowers. The petals are actually specialized flowers known as ray flowers with petals fused together into a single, strap-shaped ray. The dark center of the "sunflower" is composed of numerous small flowers known as disc flowers. The disc flowers also have petals fused together, but in this case they form a tubular corolla that is radially symmetrical. The sepals of both the ray and the disc flowers are modified into scales or bristles and are referred to as the pappus. Members of this family are confusing to the beginner, but as this is the largest family of flowering plants, it is important to gain some understanding of the flower structure of this group. For a more detailed discussion of flower structure and plant family characteristics, the reader is urged to consult a good textbook in plant taxonomy.

Technical terminology was avoided where possible, but accuracy and precision required the use of a few technical terms. Those used to describe the shapes of leaves are illustrated in Figure II, page xvii. The glossary that follows includes all other technical terms used in this book.

Interest in natural history, conservation, and particularly wildflowers has grown significantly in recent years. The emergence and continued growth of such organizations as The Alabama Conservancy and, more recently, the Alabama Wildflower Society is evidence that this interest is more than just a fad. The authors are hopeful that this book will further stimulate this growing enthusiasm in the study, enjoyment, and, above all, conservation of the beautiful wildflowers of Alabama.

ACKNOWLEDGMENTS

The authors would like to express appreciation to the many who have helped make this book possible. First, special thanks is extended to those who placed orders in advance and have waited so long for the book, including particularly members of the Federated Garden Clubs of Alabama, the Alabama Wildflower Society, the Birmingham Botanical Society, and the Birmingham Audubon Society.

Special appreciation is due James H. Hancock and Robert R. Reid, Jr., who helped in so many ways.

Several persons were helpful in providing information on certain plants, including particularly the following: the late Dr. R.M. Harper for help with many identifications, including *Andrachne phyllanthoides*; Dr. C.L. Rogers for help with orchids; Dr. Frank McCormick for help with *Arenaria*; Dr. John D. Freeman for help with *Trillium*; Dr. E.T. Wherry for help with *Phlox*; Mrs. Lindsay C. (Weesie) Smith for help with *Erythronium*, *Hexastylis*, and *Trillium*; Mrs. Harriet Wright for help with the lilies; Dr. M. LeLong and Mrs. Verda Horn for identifying *Paronychia*.

Numerous others provided valuable assistance such as collecting slides and encouraging advance sales. Especially we would like to thank Miss Amilea Porter, Mr. W.R.J. Dunn, Jr., Mrs. Helen Kittinger, Mrs. Dolly Stack, and Mr. Fairly Chandler. For great help in typing the manuscript we would like to thank Mrs. Betty Graham, Mrs. Mary Bailey, and Mrs. Polly Cobb.

A very special acknowledgment is due to Dr. James H. Mason and to Mrs. Marly Thomas, without whose assistance, patience, and understanding this book would not have been possible.

A most valuable part of the book is the result of the photographers' work. In addition to the photographs made by the authors, this book includes photographs made by others who spent many hours carrying heavy equipment into the field and waiting for the proper conditions of light or for changes in the wind or cloud cover. We give special thanks to these photographers: Rebecca Bray, Mary Burks, Fairly Chandler, Bob Cobb, Harold Cooley, Fred Fish, Mike Hopiak, Helen

Kittinger, Dock Loyd, Louise McSpadden, James D. Mason, Bob Mills, Ruth Monasco, John Scott, Dolly Stack, and Harriet Wright. In the Photographic Credits immediately following the plant descriptions, there is a list of the photographers and the plants that they photographed for inclusion in this book.

The authors and publishers wish particularly to thank all the individuals and organizations whose financial support made it possible to publish this book. These gracious sponsors are listed preceding the Index, with the exception of a few who wish to remain anonymous.

Flower and Leaf Arrangements

FLOWER PARTS

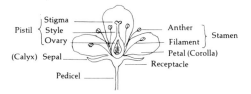

Pistil { Stigma, Style, Ovary
(Calyx) Sepal
Pedicel
Anther, Filament } Stamen
Petal (Corolla)
Receptacle

FLOWER TYPES

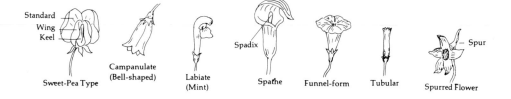

Standard, Wing, Keel
Sweet-Pea Type

Campanulate (Bell-shaped)

Labiate (Mint)

Spadix
Spathe

Funnel-form

Tubular

Spur
Spurred Flower

INFLORESCENCES

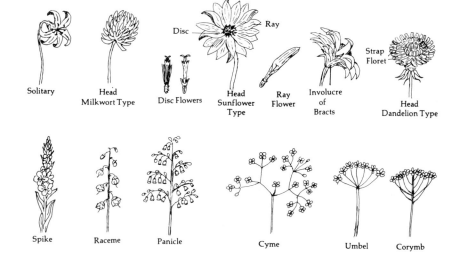

Solitary

Head Milkwort Type

Disc Flowers

Disc
Head Sunflower Type
Ray

Ray Flower

Involucre of Bracts

Strap Floret
Head Dandelion Type

Spike

Raceme

Panicle

Cyme

Umbel

Corymb

Figure I

LEAF ARRANGEMENTS

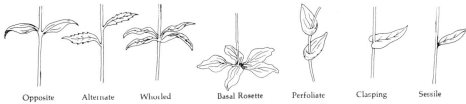

Opposite   Alternate   Whorled   Basal Rosette   Perfoliate   Clasping   Sessile

LEAF DIVISIONS

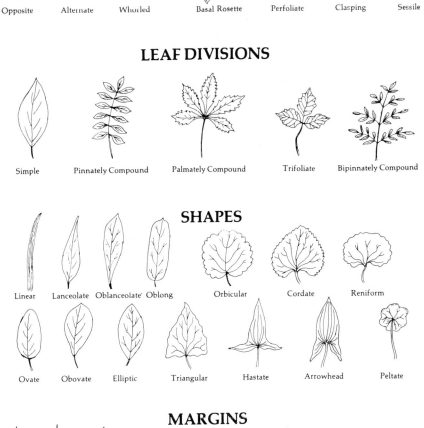

Simple   Pinnately Compound   Palmately Compound   Trifoliate   Bipinnately Compound

SHAPES

Linear   Lanceolate   Oblanceolate   Oblong   Orbicular   Cordate   Reniform

Ovate   Obovate   Elliptic   Triangular   Hastate   Arrowhead   Peltate

MARGINS

Entire   Dentate   Serrate   Crenate   Wavy   Pinnately Lobed   Palmately Lobed   Cleft

Figure II

GLOSSARY

achene   A small, hard, dry, non-splitting fruit with one seed.

annual   A plant that completes its life cycle in one year or less.

anther   The upper, enlarged part of a stamen that contains the pollen.

axil   The upper angle where the leaf joins the stem.

barbed   Furnished with rigid points or short bristles.

beaked   Ending in a beak or prolonged tip.

biennial   A plant that completes its life cycle in two years; it blooms the second year.

bisexual flower   A flower that contains both stamens and pistils. This is often referred to as a perfect flower.

blade   The flat, expanded part of a leaf.

bract   A leaflike structure associated with a single flower or group of flowers, differing in size, shape, color, or any combination of these from the other leaves of the plant.

bristle   A stiff hair or similar outgrowth.

bulb   An underground stem bearing numerous fleshy or scaly leaves, as in an onion.

bulbil   A bulblike body, especially one borne on a stem or the flowering part of a plant.

calyx   The outermost cycle of flower parts, composed of sepals, usually green and leaflike but sometimes like petals; the sepals may be separate or joined.

capsule   A dry, multiple-seeded fruit that opens or splits along two or more lines when mature.

ciliate   Hairy along the margin.

clawed   Narrowed at the base into a thin, stalklike arm.

cleft   Cut at least halfway or more from the margin to the midrib, or from the apex to the base.

cleistogamous flower   A flower that never opens, and is thus self-pollinating.

compound   Made up of two or more similar parts.

cordate   Heart-shaped.

corm   An enlarged, fleshy, more or less spherical underground base of a stem.

corolla   The inner part of the flower, made up of petals. The petals may be separated or united and may be of any color.

creeping   Growing flat on or beneath the ground and rooting.

crested   Bearing an elevated appendage like a crest.

deciduous   Falling away at the end of the growing period or shedding leaves at the end of the growing period; not evergreen.

decumbent   Reclining, but with the tips ascending.

deflexed   Bent downward from the tip.

dentate   Toothed, especially with outwardly projecting teeth.

dioecious   Having unisexual flowers, with male and female flowers on separate plants.

disc   In the Asteraceae or Sunflower Family, the central part of the flower head, bearing many small tubular flowers.

disc flower   One of the tubular flowers in the disc of a flower head of the Asteraceae or Sunflower Family.

dissected   Divided many times; cut into numerous segments.

downy   Covered with short, fine hairs.

elliptic   In leaves, shaped like an ellipse, oblong with regularly rounded ends.

entire   Not interrupted by lobes or cuts; continuous, as a leaf margin without teeth, lobes, or divisions.

fertile   Capable of producing seed or viable pollen.

filament   The stalk of the stamen that supports the anther.

fruit   The seed-bearing product of a plant.

glabrous   Smooth; not hairy.

glandular   Bearing glands or exuding a sticky substance.

glaucous   Covered with a fine, white, powdery coating.

globose   Globe-shaped; somewhat spherical.

halberd-shaped   Like an arrowhead, but with basal lobes diverging hastate. See Figure II, page *xvii*, for illustration of a hastate leaf.

head   A dense cluster of flowers without stalks or on very short stems.

herb   A plant with no persistent woody stem above ground.

hirsute   With firm or stiff hairs.

incomplete flower   A flower with one or more kinds of floral parts missing. The missing parts may be sepals, petals, stamens, or pistils.

inferior ovary   The ovary of a flower in which the sepals are fused to the ovary for more than half its length.

inflated   Distended or swollen by or as if by air.

inflorescence   The flower cluster of a plant.

involucre   A circle or collection of bracts surrounding a flower. (Especially in the Sunflower Family.)

irregular   Applied to a flower in which one or more of the organs of the same series are unlike the rest. Bilaterally symmetrical.

keel   A ridge like the keel of a boat. Also, the structure formed by the two joined lower petals of a sweet-pea-type flower. (See illustration, page *xvi.*)

labiate   With lips, as the two-lipped corolla of many mints.

lanceolate   In a leaf blade, long and narrow and tapering to a point; broadest near the base.

leaflet   A single division of a compound leaf.

legume   A simple, single-compartmented fruit opening along two sides, as in the Bean Family.

lip   One of a two-lipped corolla or calyx. In a bilaterally symmetrical flower with joined petals or sepals, the upper or lower part of the corolla or calyx. The odd petal in an orchid flower.

midrib   The main vein of a leaf.

monoecious   Having unisexual flowers, with male and female flowers on the same plant.

nerve   A simple vein or slender rib.

node   The place on a stem where one or more leaves are produced.

oblanceolate   Lanceolate, but with the broadest part toward the apex; inverted lanceolate.

oblong   Longer than wide, with sides nearly parallel or somewhat curving.

obovate   Egg-shaped in outline, broadest above the middle or near the apex; inverted ovate.

opposite   Applied to two leaves at the same node, on opposite sides of the stem.

oval   Broadly elliptic.

ovary   The lower part of the pistil, where the seeds develop.

ovate   Egg-shaped in outline, with the broader end toward the base.

palmate   Lobed or divided so as to radiate from one point, as the fingers from the palm of the hand.

panicle   A loose, elongate cluster of flowers, branched several times.

pappus   The highly modified calyx of flowers of the Asteraceae or Sunflower Family. It is borne on the apex of the ovary.

parasite   A plant that gets its food from another living organism.

pedicel   The stalk of a single flower in a cluster.

peduncle   A stalk that bears either a solitary flower or a flower cluster.

perennial   A plant of three or more years duration.

perfect flower   A bisexual flower; one containing both stamens and pistils.

perfoliate   Applied to a sessile leaf or bract whose base completely surrounds the stem so that the stem seems to pass through the leaf or bract.

perianth   The corolla and calyx of a flower.

petal   One of the parts that compose the corolla.

petiole   The stalk of a leaf.

pinnate   Compound, with the leaflets on opposite sides of a common rachis.

pistil   The female reproductive organ of a flower, composed of the stigma, style, and ovary.

plumose   Feathery. Specifically, bearing fine, spreading hairs.

pod   A dry fruit that splits open along two sides at maturity.

pollen   The fertilizing grains borne in the anthers.

prostrate   Lying flat upon the ground.

pubescent   Hairy. Specifically, bearing short, downlike hairs.

raceme   A simple, elongate cluster of stalked flowers, arranged singly along a central stalk.

ray   The branch of an umbel. Also, a marginal strap-shaped flower in the Sunflower Family.

reflexed   Bent back or downward.

rhizome   A horizontal underground stem, often thick and short.

rootstock   An underground stem.

rosette   A basal cluster of leaves in a circular form, as in a dandelion.

saprophyte   A plant that gets its food from dead organic matter.

seed   The ripened ovule.

sepal   A division of the calyx.

serrated   Having sharp teeth that point forward.

sessile   Without a stalk.

sheath   A tubular envelope.

simple   Of one piece; not compound.

spadix   A thick, club-shaped stalk bearing small, crowded, stalkless flowers, as in the Arum Family.

spathe   A hooded or leaflike sheath partly enclosing the spadix, as in the Arum Family. In certain other plants, a leaflike structure at the base of a flower or flower cluster.

spatulate   Referring to leaves, spoon-shaped, narrowed downward from a rounded summit.

spike   An elongate flower cluster in which sessile flowers are arranged along a central stem.

stamen   The male reproductive organ of a flower, composed of the anther and the filament.

standard   The broad, upper petal of a flower of the Bean Family.

sterile   Unproductive. Without stamens or pistils.

stigma   The terminal part of the pistil, which receives the pollen.

stipule   An outgrowth from the base of a leaf, usually occurring in pairs, one from either side of the leaf base.

stolon   Any basal branch inclined to root.

style   The part of the pistil between the stigma and the ovary.

taproot   The main, descending root of a plant.

tendril   A slender, coiling organ of a climbing plant, used for twining about a support.

terminal   Borne at the tip of a stem or stalk.

toothed   A nontechnical term referring to leaf margins that bear projections or indentations. See Figure II, page *xvii*, for more precise illustrations of types of leaf margins.

trifoliate   Bearing three leaflets.

tuber   A thick, short, underground stem, possessing buds or "eyes."

unisexual flower   A flower that contains only one kind of sex organ, either stamens or pistils.

umbel   A flower cluster, usually flat or convex, in which all the flower stalks arise from one point. In a compound umbel, small umbels grow at the end of each of the radiating stems.

vein   A thread of fibrous conducting tissue in a leaf or other organ.

weed   A plant that aggressively invades areas of cultivation or other disturbance. Used particularly to refer to obnoxious or unwanted plants.

whorl   An arrangement of three or more leaves or flowers in a circle about a stem, all attached at a single node.

wing   A thin, rigid membrane, extending from the surface of a stem, leaf stalk, fruit, or seed. Also, one of the lateral petals of a flower of the Bean Family.

woolly   Bearing soft, curly, sometimes tangled hairs.

Descriptions of the Wildflowers

Cattail Family

Typhaceae

COMMON CATTAIL, BROAD-LEAVED CATTAIL

Typha latifolia L.

Throughout North America, Europe, and Asia in fresh-water marshes, ponds, and ditches, the cattail is a familiar sight. In late spring olive-green leaves appear on stems up to 9 feet tall, growing in dense ranks studded by brown flower heads. These cylindrical spikes appear bicolored and divided into two parts. The upper, pollen-bearing half consists of yellow-brown stamens. The lower half bears minute female flowers and after fertilization develops into the familiar cattail. The seedlike fruit bears long hairs that aid in dispersal. The large, underground rhizome is starchy and edible. May—July. Throughout eastern U.S. and into Can. The narrow-leaved cattail, *Typha angustifolia* is similar but has narrower leaves and a distinct separation between the male and female flowers.

Bur Reed Family

Sparganiaceae

BUR REED

Sparganium americanum Nutt.

Bur reeds are marsh or aquatic plants with thin, irislike leaves and globular flower heads forming bristly balls. Borne on the upper part of the stem, the small male flowers are shed soon after reaching maturity. The female flowers mature into hard-beaked fruits that are burlike—thus, the common name bur reed. May—September. Streams and shallow ponds from the mountains to the Coastal Plain. Ga.—Ala., north into Can.

Water Plaintain Family

Alismataceae

ARROWHEAD, DUCK POTATO

Sagittaria falcata Pursh

The arrowheads form a large group of aquatic and marsh plants, most of which have leaves shaped like an arrowhead. They grow to a height of about 4 feet and have white-petaled flowers arranged in whorls of 3's along the flowering stem. Usually the lower flowers in the cluster are female and the upper flowers are male, but occasionally the lower flowers will contain both stamens and pistils. June—October. Throughout the U.S. in swamps, pond margins, and sluggish streams. The species illustrated, *Sagittaria falcata*, is found primarily on the outer Coastal Plain, often in brackish water.

GRASS FAMILY

Poaceae

SEA OATS, BEACH GRASS

Uniola paniculata L.

The grasses constitute one of the largest families of flowering plants, but this book illustrates only one species—one very much in need of protection to save it from extinction. Sea oats is a stout, pale green perennial with an extensive system of rhizomes and roots that aid in stabilizing beach sands. Flowers are produced in large arching panicles of golden spikelets on stems 6—10 feet high. The panicles dry and remain on the plant throughout the winter, and although very decorative in dried arrangements, they should never be collected. In most states there is a heavy fine for gathering sea oats. August—September. Along the coast on sandhills. Ala.—Tex., north to Va.

Common Cattail

Bur Reed

Arrowhead

Sea Oats

Sedge Family Cyperaceae

WHITETOP SEDGE, STAR RUSH *Dichromena colorata* (L.) Hitchc.

Unlike most members of the sedge family, whitetop produces a showy inflorescence with bracts that resemble flowers. The true flowers are minute and hidden in the scales of small spikelets clustered tightly at the tips of the triangular stems. The inconspicuous flowers are surrounded by 6 or fewer drooping white bracts tipped with green. Whitetop is commonly associated with pitcher plants and sundews and is easily recognized at a considerable distance. The white bracts are in evidence from January through August. Marshes and salt flats, outer Coastal Plain. Fla.—Tex., north to Va. A related species, *Dichromena latifolia*, is perhaps even more showy with seven or more wide flowering bracts.

Arum Family Araceae

GOLDEN CLUB, BOG TORCH *Orontium aquaticum* L.

In early spring the golden clubs bloom along the shallow waters of coastal and inland ponds and swamps. The long stems whiten and thicken into the 8—16-inch clubs or spadices, each bearing at the tip tiny golden-yellow flowers. The spathe is a small sheathing leaf at the base of the stem. The stems stand erect in flower, prostrate in fruit. The leaves are in a basal cluster covered with an iridescent, grayish film that repels water, explaining one of the local names, never-wet. March—April. Acid bogs and shallow streams. Fla.—Tex., north to Mass.

WHITE ARUM, SPOONFLOWER *Peltandra sagittaefolia* (Michx.) Morong.

White arum is very rare, being found only in acid bogs of the Southern Coastal Plain. The white spathe spreads at the top and resembles that of a calla lily. The upper portion of the spadix bears male flowers and the lower portion, enclosed in the tube, bears female flowers. June—August. Ga.—Miss., north to N.C. The green arum, *Peltandra virginica*, has a much wider range and is distinguished by green berries and a green spathe that completely covers the spadix.

JACK-IN-THE-PULPIT, INDIAN TURNIP *Arisaema triphyllum* (L.) Schott

Jack-in-the-pulpit is a perennial that grows in deep rich woods. The 3-parted leaves rise above the canopied bloom. The spathe, a modified leaf, is the pulpit that arches over the spadix (Jack) in which tiny flowers are embedded. A single spadix usually bears either male or female flowers, but occasionally both kinds are borne on a single spadix. The berries are brilliant scarlet. The underground stem consists of corms containing crystals of calcium oxalate that burn the mouth. Indians learned to remove this substance by boiling and often ate these corms. March—April. Low woods, bogs. Ga.—La., north to Mass.

Whitetop Sedge

White Arum

Golden Club

Jack-in-the-Pulpit

5

Yellow-eyed Grass Family   Xyridaceae

YELLOW-EYED GRASS   *Xyris baldwiniana* R. & S.

Several species in the genus *Xyris* have the same common name and are very difficult to distinguish. All have yellow flowers in compact, terminal, headlike spikes. Each flower is subtended by a woody scale that covers the flower bud and later the fruit. One or two flowers emerge each day but are quickly shed. Although not true grasses, these plants have grasslike leaves in tufted clumps. June—July. Bogs and swamps on the Coastal Plain. Fla., Ga., Ala., Miss.

Pipewort Family   Eriocaulaceae

PIPEWORT, HATPIN   *Eriocaulon decangulare* L.

Near the coast the white, gray, and tan heads of pipeworts stud the roadside ditches and shallow marshes. The monoecious plants have flowers in dense heads that are hard and covered with long soft hairs. The male flowers have 4—6 stamens per flower, and the female flowers have stalked ovaries. June—October. Bogs, wet pinelands, mountains and Coastal Plain. Ga.—Miss., north to Va. *Eriocaulon compressum* is very similar but is dioecious, whereas *E. lineare* is monoecious and has smaller flower heads.

Spiderwort Family   Commelinaceae

DAYFLOWER   *Commelina erecta* L.

Plants of the genus *Commelina* are delicate perennial herbs with erect stems and lanceolate leaves up to 6 inches long. The leaves sheath the stem, and the sheathing portion bears hairs along the margin. Flower clusters are borne inside a bract that is folded lengthwise forming a spathe. The flowers open one at a time and are very short-lived, remaining open for only one morning. In *C. erecta*, the two upper petals are blue, erect, and more conspicuous than the much smaller, white or translucent, third petal. April—October. Common and widespread, often weedy. Fla.—Tex., north to N.Y. and Kan.

VIRGINIA SPIDERWORT   *Tradescantia virginiana* L.

The spiderworts are handsome plants of woods, meadows, stream banks, and road-sides. From a large cluster of buds formed in the axils of the leaflike bracts, one or two showy blue to purple flowers open each morning and close by noon. The flowers have 3 sepals, 3 petals, and 6 stamens. The golden anthers borne on bearded filaments are conspicuous. March—May. Woods, fields, roadsides, and waste places. Ga.—Ala., north to Conn. and Wis.

Yellow-eyed Grass

Pipewort

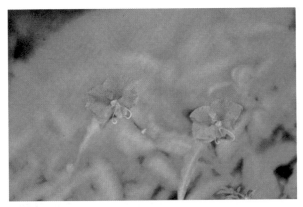

Dayflower

Virginia Spiderwort

7

HAIRY SPIDERWORT   *Tradescantia hirsuticaulis* Small

Hairy spiderwort is a perennial herb that is densely hairy along the stem and to a lesser extent on the leaves. Lanceolate in form, the leaves are up to 10 inches long and taper to long, thin points. The sepals are distinctive, bearing two kinds of hairs, some with and some without glandular tips. The petals vary from blue to rose-pink and are about ¾ of an inch long. April—June. Dry, sandy soil in woods and along rocky ledges. Fla.—Ala., north to N.C.

Pickerelweed Family   Pontederiaceae

PICKERELWEED, WAMPEE   *Pontederia cordata* L.

Pickerelweed is a large aquatic plant, growing 2—3½ feet high from a short, thick rhizome. The leaves are basal, ovate to lanceolate, with a heart-shaped base. Standing a foot or more above the water, the flower spike bears 2 bracts; the upper is a small papery sheath just below the spike, and the lower is heart-shaped, resembling the basal leaves. The perianth is violet-blue, rarely white, with a yellow upper lobe. Each flower lasts only one day but is replaced each day so that there is a progression of blooms from the base to the apex of the spike. May—October. Along muddy shores and quiet waters. Ga., Fla., Miss., north into Can.

WATER HYACINTH   *Eichhornia crassipes* (Mart.) Solms.

The rounded leaves of the water hyacinth have hollow petioles with a spongy, inflated base that buoys the plant. The roots hang in a fibrous mass below the floating top. The perianth is 2-lipped with the upper lip 3-lobed and blotched with blue and yellow. The blooms last only one day, but a continual procession of blossoms occurs from early spring to late fall. Introduced from South America, the water hyacinth has spread rampantly in this country and is now a menace, choking streams, ditches, and estuaries. So far, no satisfactory measures have been found to control this beautiful but worrisome species. Fla.—Tex., north to Va.

Lily Family   Liliaceae

FAIRY WAND, BLAZING STAR   *Chamaelirium luteum* (L.) Gray

In dark woods the white spires of the fairy wand seem to glisten. The slender flowering stems are 1—3 feet high with leaves both in a basal rosette and along the stems. The small white flowers are borne on tightly packed racemes or spikes 3—9 inches long. The male and female flowers are on separate plants, the female flowers usually more greenish than the male flowers. The fruit is a 3-chambered capsule bearing reddish seeds. March—May. Infrequent in moist woods and bogs. Fla.—Miss. and Ark., north to Mass. and Mich.

Hairy Spiderwort

Pickerelweed

Water Hyacinth

Fairy Wand

White Featherling   *Tofieldia glabra* Nutt.

The flowers of white featherling are borne in racemes and are very small and dainty. The stems and leaves are glabrous and smooth to touch. A closely related species, *Tofieldia racemosa*, has rough stems. August—October. Open pineland of the Coastal Plain, often growing with pitcher plants and sundews. Ga.—Ala., north to N.C.

Fly-Poison   *Amianthium muscaetoxicum* (Walt.) Gray

This plant is a perennial growing from a bulb and bearing flowers on a bare stem 1½—4 feet tall. Broadly linear, the leaves are a foot or more in length. The flowers are in a dense terminal raceme 2—6 inches long. The small petals are white at maturity but persist and become green or purplish with age. The plant contains a very toxic alkaloid, and all parts are considered poisonous. A sugar solution that includes one of the crushed bulbs is supposed to attract and kill flies. May—July. Low sandy grounds, bogs, open woods. Ga.—Okla., north to Pa.

Bunchlily, Bunchflower   *Melanthium virginicum* L.

The common name bunchlily refers to the manner in which the flowers are bunched or crowded together into a panicle of racemes that may be 12 inches high and 8 inches wide. The flowers are creamy white but turn blackish as they age. The scientific name *Melanthium* is from the Greek meaning "black flower." Slightly more than ¼ inch long, the persistent sepals and petals are narrow and clawed at the base. June—August. Bogs, wet woods. Fla.—Tex., north to N.Y. and Minn.

Featherbells, Featherfleece   *Stenanthium gramineum* (Ker) Morong.

The flower cluster of featherbells is a panicle of racemes 2 feet long resembling large white feathers. Downward-slanting flower branches are borne on stems that are 3—6 feet high. Resembling small stars, the flowers have pointed petals that are greenish-white or purplish and about ½ inch long. The fruit is a small 3-beaked pod. The leaves are mainly basal, very narrow, and folded lengthwise. July—September. Rich dry woods, thickets, meadows. Ga., Fla., to Tenn., Ky., Va., and W. Va.

White Featherling

Bunchlily

Fly-Poison

Featherbells

CROW-POISON, BLACK SNAKEROOT   *Zigadenus densus* (Desr.) Fern.

The white flowers of *Zigadenus* resemble those of *Amianthium* and likewise are poisonous. They are borne in thick, candlelike racemes that on close examination resemble plumes. There are two small glands at the base of the perianth that are usually missing in dried specimens. The plant grows from a bulb to a height of 2–3 feet and bears 1–3 narrow, linear basal leaves. April—early June. Moist pinelands and bogs. Fla.—Tex., north to Va. *Zigadenus glaberrimus* is a coarser plant growing from a clumped, creeping rhizome.

SUNNYBELLS   *Schoenolirion croceum* (Michx.) Gray

This bulbous perennial herb has smooth, leafless stems that grow to a height of about one foot. Borne in a panicle of racemes, the flowers are bright yellow and each is subtended by a thick, translucent bract. The fruit is a 2-chambered capsule with 2 lustrous black seeds in each chamber. April—May. Sandy soil, moist pinelands and swamps. Ga., Fla., N.C.

RECURVED-SEPAL TRILLIUM   *Trillium recurvatum* Beck

All members of the genus *Trillium* are perennial herbs of spring, growing from a short rhizome and bearing a single terminal flower. This species and the following four have sessile flowers. Three distinct characteristics will help identify *T. recurvatum*, which is rare in Alabama; the leaves have petioles, the sepals are strongly recurved, and the rhizome is long and slender. The stem is 6–18 inches high, and the purplish-brown petals are short and curve gracefully inward at the top. April—May. Northwest Ala., to western Ark. and Tex. north to Minn. and Ohio. A similar species, *T. lancifolium*, with very narrow petals, is found in the mountains of Ala., Ga., and Fla.

TRAILING TRILLIUM   *Trillium decumbens* Harbison

One of the earliest flowering species of *Trillium*, *T. decumbens*, is a true harbinger of spring. In the moist rocky woods of Alabama the trailing trillium unfolds its white and green mottled leaves in February. Because of its decumbent stem, the leaves rest on the ground. By mid May the plants have died down for the year. February—March. Mountains. Ga.—Ala.

Crow-Poison

Sunnybells

Recurved-Sepal Trillium

Trailing Trillium

TWISTED TRILLIUM   *Trillium stamineum* Harbison

This species is easy to identify by the twisted purple-brown petals that spread to horizontal during flowering, and by a disagreeable odor with age. The leaves are lightly mottled and held on stems 6—20 inches high. It is fairly common in middle and western Ala. March—April. Coastal Plain. Ga.—Miss. and Tenn.

WHIPPOORWILL-FLOWER, LITTLE SWEET BETSY   *Trillium cuneatum* Raf.

If unable to identify a sessile trillium in the northern half of Alabama, it is probably *Trillium cuneatum* because this is the most common and variable species in the state. The stems are 4—18 inches tall, with leaves dully mottled green and brown. The sessile flower has petals that are 3—4 times as long as wide. Normally purple, the flower may also be light brown, greenish, or rarely, yellow. April—early June. Central and north Ala., Ky., N.C. A closely related species, *T. maculatum*, grows on the Coastal Plain of Ala.

UNDERWOOD'S TRILLIUM   *Trillium underwoodii* Small

The leaves of this Coastal Plain species are up to 8 inches long, are beautifully mottled in 3 or more shades of green, and have a velvety sheen. The stems are only 6—10 inches tall, so the leaves often dip to the ground. The maroon petals are long and narrow; the green sepals are more than half the length of the petals. Scattered localities on the Coastal Plain, primarily wooded slopes. Fla., Ala., Ga.

BENT TRILLIUM   *Trillium flexipes* Raf.

This species and the following three have flowers borne on distinct stalks. *Trillium flexipes* is a large handsome trillium with a delicate scent and grows in the Cumberland Plateau region of Alabama in scattered colonies where the plants are often locally abundant. Unusually tall for a trillium, this species reaches a height of 10—24 inches and has large, light green leaves. Borne on tall flowering stalks, the flowers have petals that vary from white to reddish-purple. The ovary and anthers are cream-colored or white. April. Cumberland Plateau. Ala., Tenn., Ky.

Twisted Trillium

Whippoorwill-Flower

Underwood's Trillium

Bent Trillium

Nodding Trillium
Trillium cernuum L.

Because of its strongly recurved pedicel, the small white flower of the nodding trillium hangs under the large, light green, unmottled leaves. The stems are 12—18 inches tall. The petals and filaments are white; the anthers, purple-tipped; and the ovary, lavender. The rhizome is short, 1¼—2¼ inches long. April—early May. Moist woods. Central and northern Ala., Ga., north to Va.

Catesby's Trillium
Trillium catesbaei Ell.

Catesby's trillium is distinctive in having a nodding pink or white flower with yellow stamens beneath elliptic, wavy, short-petioled leaves. The stems are green to purple, and the leaves are 3-nerved and not mottled. The petals are white when the buds open, but darken to almost red with age. This is one of the late blooming trilliums in Alabama. March—May. Wooded slopes and coves. Piedmont, mountains. Ala., Ga., Tenn.

Least Trillium
Trillium pusillum Michx.

This delightful little trillium with narrow, unmottled leaves is 4—8 inches tall. It is unusual in that it grows in swamps and bogs. A slender peduncle holds erect a dainty white flower that turns pink with age. The ovary is white, the anthers, yellow with purplish connectives. Late March—May. Alluvial woods, swamps. Ala., north to Va.

Indian Cucumber-Root
Medeola virginiana L.

This is an attractive perennial growing to a height of 1—3 feet from a rhizome that is edible and has the taste of cucumber. It is easily identified by two whorls of leaves a few inches apart on the stem. The lower whorl has 6—10 leaves, the upper whorl has only 3—4 leaves that are much smaller. Greenish-yellow with purple stamens, the flowers are sessile in the axils of the upper whorl of leaves. It is lovely and easily grown in home flower gardens. April—June. Rich soil. Fla. to La., north to Can.

Nodding Trillium

Catesby's Trillium

Least Trillium

Indian Cucumber-Root

COLICROOT, STAR GRASS

Aletris farinosa L.

The white tubular corolla of *Aletris* has a mealy texture; thus, the genus was named for the legendary slave girl Aletris who ground grain. The pointed leaves form a basal rosette from which arises a flowering stem that is 1—3 feet tall and has reduced leaves or is leafless. The small, cylindrical, white flowers are approximately ½ inch long. April—June. Moist meadows, bogs, ditches. Coastal Plain. Ga.—Miss., north to Me. and Wis. *Aletris aurea* is a later flowering species with golden-yellow flowers. Species of *Aletris* are found only in eastern North America and eastern Asia.

TWISTED-STALK

Streptopus amplexifolius (L.) DC.

A stoloniferous perennial herb from a short thick rhizome, *Streptopus* is a wide-ranging genus with species throughout the cooler portions of the Northern Hemisphere. The greenish flowers do not emerge from the stem at the point at which the buds are formed. Rather, the flower stalk remains fused to the stem for some distance, and the flowers often appear to emerge from just below a leaf instead of from the leaf axil. The flower stalk bends abruptly downward at the tip, bearing a single flower or fruit. The name *Streptopus* means "twisted foot" and refers to this bending or twisting. July—August. Damp woods, mountains. Ala., Ga., north to N.Y. and Alaska.

SOLOMON'S SEAL

Polygonatum biflorum (Walt.) Ell.

This perennial herb with an elongated white rhizome is one of the most common species of Southern woodlands. The arching stems are 1—3 feet tall with broad, ribbed leaves and 2 or more creamy white flowers in small clusters hanging under the curved stem. A characteristic bract subtending each flower cluster sheaths the stem below the leaves. In a related species, *Polygonatum pubescens*, this bract is usually missing, leaving a scar that nearly circles the stem. Late April—June. Moist woodlands. Fla.—Tex., north to Conn. and southern Ont.

FALSE SOLOMON'S SEAL, FALSE SPIKENARD

Smilacina racemosa (L.) Desf.

A graceful pubescent plant resembling Solomon's Seal, *Smilacina* is easily distinguished by its white flowers clustered into a terminal inflorescence consisting of a panicle of racemes. The blue-green leaves are elliptic, lance-shaped, and short-petioled. The fruit is a berry that is green at first, becomes yellow speckled with brown, and eventually turns a beautiful translucent red. April—June. Moist deciduous forests. Ga.—Miss., north into Can.

Twisted-Stalk

Colicroot

Solomon's Seal

False Solomon's Seal

YELLOW MANDARIN, FAIRY-BELLS   *Disporum lanuginosum* (Michx.) Nicholson

This low herbaceous perennial is distinguished by the bell-shaped flowers borne in 2's or 3's at the tips of the branches. The long, pointed, sessile leaves are hairy along the margins and usually on the lower surface. The greenish petals and sepals, nearly an inch in length, are clearly longer than the stamens. The fruit is a smooth red berry. April—May. Dense woods. Ga.—Ala., north to N.Y. and Ont.

WILD HYACINTH   *Camassia scilloides* (Raf.) Cory

Camassia is a smooth perennial with an edible bulb and a naked stem that grows to a height of 8 inches to 2 feet. The small showy flowers are pale blue, lavender, or white and are borne in terminal racemes. Sepals and petals are ½ inch long. The fruit is a 3-chambered capsule, broader than long. This attractive plant is easily grown from seeds and is commonly cultivated. April—May. Wet woods and thickets. Ga.—Tex., north to Pa., southern Ont.

GRAPE HYACINTH   *Muscari racemosum* (L.) Mill.

Native to the Mediterranean region, species of *Muscari* have become thoroughly naturalized and widespread in the U.S. A bulbous perennial, *M. racemosum* has a leafless stem 2—10 inches tall. The leaves are narrow and almost round in cross section. The small blue flowers are oval in outline and borne in dense, bell-like, bracted racemes, resembling bunches of grapes. March—April. Old fields, lawns, roadsides. Ga.—Ala., north to Mass. A related species, *M. botryoides*, is distinguished by its flat leaves and globular perianth.

TROUT LILY, DOGTOOTH VIOLET   *Erythronium rostratum* Wolf

From a pair of shiny, mottled leaves on a stem 2—6 inches high, the yellow flower of the trout lily appears in early spring. Only plants that bear a pair of leaves produce flowers; those with one leaf do not bloom. The flowers are 1—1½ inches across, solitary, and nodding, but the pedicel straightens with age and holds the fruit erect. February—April. Rich woods and ravines, primarily in the mountains and Piedmont. Ga.—Miss. Related species occurring in Alabama include *Erythronium americanum*, which has pendant fruits, and *E. umbilicatum*, which has deeply lobed fruits and is not stoloniferous.

Yellow Mandarin

Wild Hyacinth

Grape Hyacinth

Trout Lily

WHITE TROUT LILY
Erythronium albidum Nutt.

Very rare in Alabama, the white trout lily is known from one limestone hillside in the Tennessee Valley and from Cullman County. The flowers are about 1¼ inches across and have white petals. This species is distributed primarily in the Mississippi Valley. *Erythronium albidum* is sometimes confused with white-flowered forms of *E. americanum* but is easily distinguished by its 3-cleft stigma. April—May. Ga.—Ky., north to Ont.

TURK'S-CAP LILY, LILY ROYAL
Lilium superbum L.

One of the largest and most freely flowering of our native lilies, the turk's-cap may have up to 25 nodding flowers on a stem 3—9 feet tall. In whorls of 5—20, the lanceolate leaves are gritty to touch along the margins and occasionally on the veins beneath. The corolla and calyx are orange to reddish with numerous dark spots on the lower half and have a narrow, starlike, wedge-shaped, green area at the base. The sepals and petals are up to 4 inches long. July—August. Rare in Alabama, found only in moist woods, meadows, and coves in the plateau region of Winston County. Ga.—Ala., north to W. Va., Va.

CAROLINA LILY
Lilium michauxii Poir.

Although strongly resembling turk's-cap, the Carolina lily is not as tall or as freely flowering and is usually found on drier sites. The stem grows from 1—4 feet high and bears 1—6 drooping, orange-red flowers with the perianth so sharply reflexed that the sepals and petals intertwine at the tips. The flowers are 2—3 inches across and densely flecked but do not have a green star at the base. The leaves are abruptly pointed and usually spatulate. August—September. Dry hillsides, mountains and Piedmont. Ga.—Fla., north to W. Va., Va.

SOUTHERN RED LILY, PINE LILY
Lilium catesbaei Walt.

The erect flower as well as the distinct color of the Southern red lily make it easy to identify. The narrow leaves are scattered along the 1—3½-foot stem. Usually solitary, the flowers are 2—3 inches across, and are red-orange to red, blotched with yellow at the base. The sepals and petals are alike, narrowed near the base to rounded stalks and tapered above to long, narrow, claw-shaped tips that curve slightly outward and downward. This beautiful lily was named for its discoverer, Mark Catesby, English naturalist and pioneer who was among the first to describe the Southeastern flora. August—September. Wet pinelands, bogs, and swamps. Ala.—La., north to Va.

White Trout Lily

Turk's-Cap Lily

Carolina Lily

Southern Red Lily

Canada Lily, Wild Yellow Lily   *Lilium canadense* L.

A wide ranging and highly variable species in the northern part of its range, the Canada lily is found only in the mountainous regions of Alabama. The corolla varies from yellow to dark orange and is heavily spotted. Up to 20 nodding flowers may be borne on a single stem. The perianth flares outward but is not reflexed, and the stamens and styles do not extend beyond the petals. June—July. Moist upland meadows and woods. Ga., Fla., north into Can.

Large-flowered Bellwort, Merrybells   *Uvularia grandiflora* J.E. Smith

The bellworts are slender-stemmed woodland plants with yellow flowers and drooping leaves at flowering time. The large-flowered bellwort grows 6—30 inches high on stems that are unbranched, solitary, and without underground stolons. The perfoliate leaves are elliptic, shiny, and hairy beneath. The thin stems bear 1—3 flowers almost 2 inches long with golden-yellow sepals and petals that hang bell-like and are smooth inside. April—May. Wooded coves of limestone areas, mountains. Ga.—Ala., north to Can.

Perfoliate Bellwort   *Uvularia perfoliata* L.

The perfoliate bellwort is distinctly colonial, forming interconnected patches from a long, slender, white, underground stolon. The leaves are smooth beneath and shiny above. The tan or straw-colored flowers are solitary, with the petals and sepals about an inch long and roughened on the inner surface. It is not readily apparent that the flower is axillary because a large leafy bract surrounds the flower stalk near the end and makes the flower appear terminal. March—May. Open woods, primarily in acid soil. Ga.—Fla., north to Can. Two other bellworts occur in Alabama, both of which have sessile but not perfoliate leaves. *Uvularia sessilifolia* has a bractless pedicel; *U. floridana* has a leafy bract below the flower.

Wild Onion, Cuthbert's Onion   *Allium cuthbertii* Small

The wild onions are closely related to our table onions as well as to the various alliums cultivated in flower gardens. The grasslike leaves arise from bulbs that consist largely of fleshy leaves. Cuthbert's onion has white, or rarely, pink flowers, flat leaves that are not hollow, and capsules that are crested along three lines. May—June. Coastal Plain, sandy soil. Fla.—Ala., north to N.C. A similar and more widespread species, *Allium canadense*, often has bulbils mixed with the flowers in the umbel and lacks the crested capsules.

Canada Lily

Perfoliate Bellwort

Large-flowered Bellwort

Wild Onion

FALSE GARLIC, SCENTLESS GARLIC   *Allium bivalve* (L.) Kuntze

This scentless garlic fills the landscape with small white stars in early spring, making up in numbers what it lacks in size. It is similar to other species of *Allium* but does not have a trace of the characteristic onion or garlic odor. For this reason it is often placed in a different genus *(Nothoscordum)*. One of the earliest of the spring flowers, false garlic occasionally blooms as early as February in central Alabama. February—May. Ala., Ga., Fla., north to Va.

Amaryllis Family   Amaryllidaceae

SPIDER LILY   *Hymenocallis coronaria* (Le Conte) Kunth

This rare spider lily grows from bulbs secure in the cracks between rocks in shallow water of the Cahaba River and Hatchet Creek in Alabama. Three or more fragrant flowers are borne on each stem and have crowns 2 inches or more wide, with several sharp, irregular teeth between the stamens. April—May. Shoals, Piedmont and Coastal Plain. Infrequent. Fla. to N.C. A closely related species, *Hymenocallis crassifolia*, has 1—2, rarely, 3 flowers in a cluster, the crowns being 6-sided and edged with blunt teeth between the filaments.

SPIDER LILY   *Hymenocallis occidentalis* (Le Conte) Kunth

This spider lily has flowers with a narrower crown than the above. The flower is more cuplike, and has the filaments attached to the indentations on the edge of the crown. There are 4—6 teeth on the margin between the stamens. The stem is about 2 feet high and bears glossy green leaves, 6 in a cluster. The leaves appear in winter or early spring, disappearing in early May. July—August. Moist hillsides, Piedmont, rarely Coastal Plain. Ga., north to Mo. and Ind.

ATAMASCO LILY, EASTER LILY   *Zephyranthes atamasco* (L.) Herb.

This bulbous perennial, with narrow linear leaves sheathing the base, is one of our most beautiful native species. The stems are 4—10 inches tall and bear solitary, white or pinkish flowers 2—4 inches across. The 3-lobed stigma extends slightly beyond the stamens. Easily transplanted, the atamasco lily is commonly brought into cultivation. March—April. Rich woods, particularly in calcareous soil. Lower Piedmont and Coastal Plain. Common. Ga., Fla., north to Va.

False Garlic

Spider Lily

Spider Lily

Atamasco Lily

SWAMP LILY, STRING LILY   *Crinum americanum* L.

Along the marshes and swamps of the outer Coastal Plain, the naked flowering stem of the swamp lily can be found during most of the year. From early spring to late fall, clusters of 3—5 fragrant blooms are produced with white sepals and petals 1—4 inches long. The leaves are mostly basal, with narrow, linear blades. The bulbs are fleshy. March—November. Near the coast. Fla. to Tex.

STAR GRASS   *Hypoxis hirsuta* (L.) Cov.

The narrow linear leaves of *Hypoxis* resemble those of grass, but the structure of the yellow flowers shows clearly that the plant is a member of the amaryllis family. The leaves and the naked flowering stems develop from an underground corm that is ¾ inch thick and covered by a brown sheath. In *H. hirsuta*, the flowering stems protrude from the leaf sheaths and bear 3—7 flowers in a cluster. March—October. Woods, meadows. Fla.—Tex., north to Can. *Hypoxis juncea* has very narrow, threadlike leaves and flower clusters of 1—3 flowers; *H. sessile* has flowering stems less than an inch high, and iridescent brown seeds.

FALSE ALOE   *Agave virginica* L.

The thick fleshy leaves of *Agave* are 8—16 inches long and are clustered into a basal rosette. The flowers are borne on leafless stalks up to 10 feet tall in a loose spike or raceme. The fragrance of the flowers is particularly strong at night, attracting a variety of night-flying insects as pollinating agents. The greenish perianth is 1—2 inches long and tubular for more than half its length. June—August. Dry slopes, sandy, rocky soil. Piedmont and mountains. Fla.—Tex., north to Va. In Mexico several species of *Agave* known as century plants are the source of a number of important economic products, including the fermented beverage pulque and the distilled form, mescal or tequila.

Bloodwort Family   Haemodoraceae

REDROOT   *Lachnanthes caroliniana* (Lam.) Dandy

A perennial herb up to 3 feet tall with stems that are hairy near the tip, redroot has rhizomes with a blood-red sap that was formerly used as a dye. The yellow flowers are densely clustered into coiled, terminal corymbs. Yellow to brownish in color, the sepals are covered with dingy, woolly pubescence. The protruding stamens, 3 in each flower, help to distinguish this genus from *Lophiola*. The seeds are dark brown and flattened. June—early September. Sandy savannas, ditches, bogs, often associated with pitcher plants. Coastal Plain. Ga.—Miss., north to Va.

Swamp Lily

Star Grass

False Aloe

Redroot

GOLD CREST   *Lophiola americana* (Pursh) Wood

Similar to and often growing near *Lachnanthes* in bogs and pine barrens, *Lophiola* can easily be distinguished by its 6 stamens that are shorter than the perianth. Bright yellow, the sepals and petals show through a glistening, woolly pubescence. The leaves are narrow, grasslike, mainly basal, and covered with white woolly hairs. The seeds are yellow-brown, and the roots and rhizomes brown to pale yellow and ribbed. May—June. Savannas, bogs, pine barrens. Lower Coastal Plain. Ga.—Miss., north to N. C.

Iris Family   **Iridaceae**

BLACKBERRY LILY   *Belamcanda chinensis* (L.) DC.

This native of Asia has escaped from cultivation and has become naturalized in the southeastern U.S. It grows to a height of about 3 feet with linear, sword-shaped leaves characteristic of all members of the iris family. The lilylike flowers are orange with crimson spots and bloom, one each day, from a cluster enclosed in a modified leaf known as a spathe. The fruit is a capsule that splits and folds back to reveal a cluster of shiny black seeds resembling a blackberry—thus, the common name blackberry lily. June—July. Open woods, roadsides. Ala.—Ga., north to Conn. and Neb.

BLUE-EYED GRASS   *Sisyrinchium angustifolium* Mill.

The blue-eyed grass is not a true grass, nor is it always "blue-eyed," the flower color of the various species ranging from blue to yellow or even white. The flowering stem is flat and often winged, resembling the leaves. Each flowering branch bears 1—2 spathes at the top from which 2—15 flowers emerge. Large clumps of these small-flowered plants can be spectacular in an open meadow. March—June. Common in meadows and moist, open woods. Fla.—Tex., north to Can.

WHITE BLUE-EYED GRASS   *Sisyrinchium albidum* Raf.

This species can usually be distinguished by its white or pale blue flowers, but it is also distinctive in having a pair of sessile spathes on each flowering stem. The stems are very narrow, flattened, and slightly winged. Late March—May. Woodlands, sandhills, and prairies. Ala.—La., north to Can. Related species in Alabama include *Sisyrinchium arenicola*, having conspicuous tufts of persistent, old leaf bases, and *S. brownei*, having yellow flowers.

Gold Crest

Blackberry Lily

Blue-eyed Grass

White Blue-eyed Grass

Dwarf Crested Iris

Iris cristata Ait.

The dwarf crested iris grows about 4—5 inches high from a shallow rhizome that has runners and a characteristic beadlike appearance. The leaves become 10—12 inches tall at maturity, but are only half this size when the plants are flowering. The petallike sepals have a white or yellow band in the center near the base with two crested ridges. The petals are smaller than the sepals, usually stand erect, and lack the crests. April—May. Common in rich woods, mountains and Piedmont. Ga.—Miss., north to Va. and Ind.

Dwarf Iris

Iris verna L.

This species is very similar to *Iris cristata*, but is easily distinguished by its lack of a crest on the sepals. It also has narrower leaves and rhizomes that are more densely scaly. The dwarf iris is quite fragrant, whereas the crested iris is scarcely if at all fragrant. The species illustrated is a variety of the dwarf iris known as *I. verna* var. *smalliana*, having short, stocky rhizomes and usually growing in the more upland regions in the state. Early April—May. Rich woodlands, Coastal Plain. Ala.—Ga., north to Md.

Arrowroot Family

Marantaceae

Powdery Thalia

Thalia dealbata Roscoe

A stout, aquatic or semiaquatic herb, 3—5 feet tall, this thalia can often be distinguished by its powdery or whitewashed appearance. The leaves are ovate to lanceolate with a sharp pointed apex and very long petiole. Borne in a crowded panicle, the purple flowers are bilaterally symmetrical. Sterile stamens in the flower are united and petallike, and one of them forms a distinctive purple lip. June—October. Wet ditches, swamps. Rare. Fla.—Tex., north to S.C. and Mo.

Orchid Family

Orchidaceae

Yellow Lady's-Slipper

Cypripedium calceolus L.

The lady's-slippers are among the best known of the native orchids of Alabama. A characteristic flower has two narrow petals and one highly modified petal, the saclike lip. The yellow lady's-slipper grows 12—18 inches tall with 3—5 leaves borne on the flowering stem. The sepals and lateral petals are purplish-brown or greenish, and the lip is yellow or cream-colored. There are several varieties in this species, but var. *pubescens* is the one most common in Alabama. April—May. Rich, moist woods and bogs. North Ala.—Ga., north into Can.

Dwarf Crested Iris

Powdery Thalia

Dwarf Iris

Yellow Lady's-Slipper

QUEEN'S LADY'S-SLIPPER, SHOWY LADY'S-SLIPPER   *Cypripedium reginae* Walt.

This is the largest and one of the most beautiful native orchids. Although it is a fairly common species in the Northeast, it is rare in Alabama. The hairy stem grows 1—3 feet high with ribbed leaves at the top. The sepals and lateral petals are white, and the pouch-shaped lip is a delicate pink streaked with purple. The lady's-slippers, as well as many other orchids are dependent on specific mycorrhizal fungi in the roots. For this reason transplanting orchids is difficult and generally should be avoided. May—June. Wet woods and bogs, mountains. Ala.—Ga., north into Can.

MOCCASIN FLOWER, PINK LADY'S-SLIPPER   *Cypripedium acaule* Ait.

The leafless flowering stem of the moccasin flower reaches a height of 6—12 inches, with two glandular-pubescent leaves surrounding its base. The sepals and lateral petals are greenish and often twisted. The large inflated lip, up to 2 inches long, is pink or white with purple veins. This rare species may form large colonies locally in moist woods and bogs. April—July. Ala.—Ga., north into Can.

SHOWY ORCHIS   *Orchis spectabilis* L.

The showy orchis grows to a height of 2—16 inches, producing 3—10 fragrant flowers in the axil of a large leafy bract. The sepals and two lateral petals are mauve-purple, and the flat lip is white or pale violet, with a drooping spur at the base. April—July. Rare in Ala., the showy orchis is found along streams and in rich hardwood forests. Ala.—Ga., north into Can.

GRASS PINK   *Calopogon pulchellus* (Salisb.) R. Br.

One of the most common orchids in Alabama, the grass pink is usually 1—2 feet tall but occasionally may reach a height of 4 feet. Borne in an open raceme are 4—20 flowers, varying in color from rose purple to pink to almost white. Grass pink is one of few orchids that does not rotate its flowers 180 degrees during development, so the lip of its flower is the uppermost segment of the perianth. *Calopogon* is from a Greek word meaning beautiful beard, referring to the hairs on the upright lip; these hairs are club-shaped and vary in color from purple to cream-colored, tipped with orange. April-June. Piedmont and Coastal Plain. Fla.—Tex., north into Can. *Calopogon pallidus* is distinguished by having very narrow leaves, less than ¼ inch wide; *C. barbatus* is an earlier flowering species, February—May, with a rust-red beard.

Queen's Lady's-Slipper

Moccasin Flower

Showy Orchis

Grass Pink

SHADOW-WITCH

Ponthieva racemosa (Walt.) Mohr

This rare, autumn-flowering orchid has a thick, fleshy cluster of roots from which emerge a basal rosette of elliptic to obovate leaves and a leafless flowering stem that is reddish-brown or greenish. The flowers are whitish-green with lateral petals that are somewhat triangular and asymmetrical. The clawed lip is dilated below the middle and constricted near the apex. August—October. Rich woods, stream margins, usually in calcareous soil. Ga.—Fla., north to Va.

ROSE POGONIA

Pogonia ophioglossoides (L.) Ker

One of the most abundant and widespread orchids in Alabama, this dainty perennial ranges in height from 4 inches to 2 feet and bears one solitary ovate leaf near the middle of the flowering stem. A single flower (rarely 2—3) is borne at the stem tip in the axil of a bract. The fragrant flower has bright pink or white sepals and petals. The lip is fringed with a mass of papillaelike projections for which the plant was named; *Pogonia* is from the Greek meaning beard flowers. April—June. Bogs, ditches and seepage slopes. Coastal Plain. Fla.—Tex., north to Can.

FIVE-LEAVES

Isotria verticillata (Muhl. ex Willd.) Raf.

Isotria can be distinguished even when not in flower by the circle of 5—6 leaves just below the apex of the stem. Each stem bears a single flower with narrow, almost linear sepals that are greenish-bronze and up to 2½ inches long. The lateral petals are yellow-green and shorter than the sepals; the lip is yellow-green, streaked with purple. April—July. Moist or dry, acid woods, often growing in association with *Medeola*. Rare in Ala. Fla.—Tex., north to Me.

THREE-BIRDS ORCHID

Triphora trianthophora (Sw.) Rydb.

This orchid usually has three flowers borne singly from the axils of small, ovate, clasping leaves. The common name alludes to the resemblance of these flowers to three tiny birds on the wing. The flowers vary from pink to white, with the sepals and lateral petals similar. The crinkled lip has 3 toothed lobes and 3 greenish ridges running lengthwise. *Triphora*, as well as several other species of orchids, may remain dormant in the ground for several years and then send up flowering stalks. July—September. Damp woods, neutral or acid soil. Fla.—Tex., north to Me.

Rose Pogonia

Shadow-Witch

Five-Leaves

Three-Birds Orchid

ROSEBUD ORCHID, SPREADING POGONIA — *Cleistes divaricata* (L.) Ames

This orchid is easily distinguished by the tubelike form of the solitary flower. The lateral petals and the troughlike lip are coalescent, forming a pink and white tube. The stem grows to a height of about 2 feet and bears a single elliptic leaf just above the middle, similar to that of *Pogonia*. After the flower, a long-petioled basal leaf arises from the root cluster and persists throughout the summer. May—July. Peaty, acid soil. Coastal Plain. Ala.—Fla., north to Va.

SOUTHERN TWAYBLADE, LONG-LIP TWAYBLADE — *Listera australis* Lindl.

A slender, inconspicuous plant for an orchid, the Southern twayblade is readily distinguished by the pair of opposite or subopposite leaves borne near the middle of a purplish stem. The flowers are greenish or brownish-purple, in terminal racemes. The sepals and petals are tiny, and the lip is only ½ inch long, deeply cut into two narrow lobes. April—June. Infrequent in moist woods and bogs. Fla.—Miss., north to N.C.

LILY-LEAVED TWAYBLADE, MAUVE SLEEKWORT — *Liparis lilifolia* (L.) Rich.

This twayblade grows from corms to a height of about 12 inches and has a stem that is angled and winged. Two lilylike leaves, up to 6 inches long, are borne at the base of the stem. A loose raceme bears 5 or more flowers with greenish-white sepals, madder-purple to brown petals, and a greenish spadelike lip. Each sepal has 3 prominent veins, and each petal, one. May—June. Infrequent in rich woods and floodplains. Ga.—Ala., north to N.H. A similar species, *Liparis loeselii*, is a more slender plant, having yellow-green leaves, and yellowish-green flowers, each with a short, concave lip.

GREEN ADDER'S-MOUTH — *Malaxis unifolia* Michx.

This small delicate orchid has spikelike racemes of tiny greenish-white flowers. At the time of flowering, the stem is from 4—16 inches tall and bears a single shiny ovate leaf with a clasping base. The petals are threadlike and reflexed, the lip, 3-lobed and about ⅛ inch long. As the flower matures, it rotates 180 degrees bringing the lip from an uppermost to a lowermost position. April—June. Bogs, meadows, mixed forests. Ga.—Miss., north into Can.

Rosebud Orchid

Southern Twayblade

Lily-leaved Twayblade

Green Adder's-Mouth

PUTTYROOT, ADAM-AND-EVE   *Aplectrum hyemale* (Muhl. ex Willd.) Torr.

The common names for this orchid refer to the distinctive growth pattern of the underground corm (Adam) that sends out a longitudinal underground stem producing at its tip another similar corm (Eve). In spring a naked stem arises bearing up to 15 flowers on a loose raceme. The flowers are one-half inch long, purplish-green or yellow marked with madder purple. The 3-lobed lip is white marked with magenta. May—June. Rich woods and flood plains. Ga.—Ala., north into Can.

DOWNY RATTLESNAKE PLANTAIN   *Goodyera pubescens* (Willd.) R. Br.

The rattlesnake plantains are easily distinguished by their basal cluster of blue-green to olive leaves with a distinctive white variegation. The small white flowers have a saclike lip with a wavy margin. The many-flowered raceme is downy-pubescent and cylindrical. June—August. Widespread in both evergreen and deciduous forests. Ga.—Ala., north into Can. A related species, *Goodyera repens*, has racemes with a smaller number of flowers, all borne on one side of the flowering stem.

CRESTED CORALROOT   *Hexalectris spicata* (Walt.) Barnh.

One of several native orchids that are saprophytic and completely lacking in chlorophyll, the crested coralroot is perhaps the most beautiful. The flesh-colored stems grow to a height of 2—3 feet and bear a raceme of flowers, each of which is an inch or so long. The petals are yellowish with purplish-brown striations and 5—6 distinctive ridges down the middle. July—August. Widespread in rich, pine and hardwood forests. Fla.—Tex., north to Va.

GREEN FRINGED ORCHID, RAGGED ORCHID   *Habenaria lacera* (Michx.) Lodd.

This species of *Habenaria* is distinctive in having pale greenish or yellowish-white flowers. In each flower the 3-lobed lip is deeply cut into a capillary fringe that extends for more than half the length of the lip. The plant grows to a height of 10—20 inches and has 5—9 narrow, oblong leaves 3—10 inches long. June—August. Rare. Bogs, marshes, and wet woods. Fla.—Tex., north to N.C.

Puttyroot

Crested Coralroot

Downy Rattlesnake Plantain

Green Fringed Orchid

YELLOW FRINGED ORCHID, ORANGE-PLUME   *Habenaria ciliaris* (L.) R. Br.

The yellow fringed orchid is a very handsome plant growing to a height of 2–3 feet, with long, lanceolate, slightly fleshy leaves. The large, many-flowered spike of orange or golden flowers is conspicuous. The sepals are narrow, ovate, and about ⅓ of an inch long, often covering the small, narrow petals. The lip is up to an inch long, deeply fringed with a spur extending about ⅓ of its length. July–September. Uncommon, but often locally abundant. Roadsides, bogs, swamps, and pine barrens. Fla.–Tex., north into Can. A similar species, *Habenaria cristata* has a smaller, more rounded lip with a very short spur.

SOUTHERN REIN ORCHID, PALE GREEN ORCHID   *Habenaria flava* (L.) R. Br.

This orchid varies from 6 inches to 2 feet in height and bears 2 oblong or lanceolate leaves on the stem. The fragrant yellow-green flowers are borne in a loose raceme, subtended by conspicuous bracts. The distinctive lip is ovate and only ¼ inch long with a tooth usually present on each side near the base and with a prominent tubercle in the middle near the base. The spur is slender, somewhat club-shaped, and longer than the ovary. May–September. Wet meadows and marshes, particularly in acid soil. Fla.–Tex., north to Md.

SNOWY ORCHID, WHITE REIN ORCHID   *Habenaria nivea* (Nutt.) Spreng.

A slender erect plant that grows from small tubers, the snowy orchid may reach a height of 30 inches. There are 2–3 long, narrow, pointed leaves that are distinctly keeled. This species is easily distinguished from all other species of *Habenaria* by its lip that is uppermost and lacks a fringe. The spur is different also, being horizontal rather than drooping. The many-flowered raceme is conical at the apex, bearing a dense cluster of snowy white flowers. May–September. Infrequent. Rich woods, meadows, and bogs. Fla.–Tex., north to N.J.

YELLOW FRINGELESS ORCHID   *Habenaria integra* (Nutt.) Spreng.

The yellow fringeless orchid is easily distinguished from all other species of *Habenaria* in the Southeast because it is the only yellow or orange flowered species that lacks a fringe on the lip. The plants grow to a height of 2–2½ feet with sheathing leaves 8–9 inches long at the base, becoming progressively smaller toward the apex. The flowers are lemon yellow to dull orange, in dense, many-flowered racemes. July–September. Rare. Swamps, dense woods, and pine barrens. Fla.–Tex., north to N.C.

Yellow Fringed Orchid

Snowy Orchid

Southern Rein Orchid

Yellow Fringeless Orchid

WHITE FRINGED ORCHID   *Habenaria blephariglottis* (Willd.) Hook.

The name *blephariglottis* means eyelid-tongued, referring to the distinct fringe on the lip of this species. The lip is up to ½ inch long with a basal spur up to 2 inches long. The sepals are rounded and the petals, oblong or linear, resemble those of *Habenaria ciliaris*. July–September. Meadows, marshes, and bogs. Fla.–Tex., north into Can.

WHITE FRINGELESS ORCHID, MONKEY-FACED ORCHID   *Habenaria blephariglottis* var. *integrilabia* Corr.

This is a very distinctive variety of *Habenaria blephariglottis*, easily separated by its lip that is rolled and is not fringed. The racemes are few-flowered, and the spur at the base of the lip is long and curves downward. July–August. Sphagnum bogs, peaty soil. Ala., Miss., and N.C. In Clay County, Ala., this variety can be found growing in association with the green wood orchid, *H. clavellata*.

LITTLE PEARL-TWIST   *Spiranthes grayi* Ames

The name *Spiranthes* refers to the spiral formed around the stem by the flowers of this genus. Examination of the flowers of *Spiranthes* under a hand lens will reveal even to the amateur botanist that it is a member of the orchid family. Little pearl-twist is distinguished by having a single spiral of flowers, widely spreading basal leaves, and a single, tubelike root. The tiny white flowers have a lip less than ⅛ inch long, which is crinkled and not marked. June–September. Dry fields, woods, well-drained slopes. Infrequent. Ala.–Miss., north to Mass.

OVAL LADIES'-TRESSES   *Spiranthes ovalis* Lindl.

This and the 2 following species have flowers arranged in several spiral ranks rather than in a single spiral as in the other species in Alabama. *Spiranthes ovalis* has 2–4 blunt leaves at the base and several small narrow leaves on the stem. The white flowers are borne in dense spikes, with each flower oval in outline, and approximately ⅕ inch long. The lip is ovate and widely rounded at the base with a wavy margin. August–November. Infrequent in moist woods and swamp margins. Fla.–Tex., north to Va., W. Va.

White Fringed Orchid

White Fringeless Orchid

Little Pearl-Twist

Oval Ladies'-Tresses

FRAGRANT LADIES'-TRESSES   *Spiranthes odorata* (Nutt.) Lindl.

This species is very similar to *Spiranthes ovalis*, and both are treated as varieties of *S. cernua* by some authors. *Spiranthes odorata* can be readily distinguished by its stoloniferous habit, and by the flowers' fragrance, similar to that of vanilla. The lip is ovate to rhombic in outline. July—October. Infrequent in bogs and swamps, often growing in standing water. Coastal Plain. Fla.—Tex., north to Md.

NODDING LADIES'-TRESSES   *Spiranthes cernua* (L.) Rich.

The name *cernua* refers to the nodding habit of the flowers of this species. The yellowish-white, usually fragrant flowers are arranged in several spiral rows. The sepals and petals are downy-pubescent, ¼—½ inch long, flared outward forming a bugle-shaped perianth with crisped margins. This plant is perhaps the most common *Spiranthes* in Alabama. July—November. Bogs, meadows, wet woods. Fla.—Tex., north into Can.

Lizard's-Tail Family   Saururaceae

LIZARD'S-TAIL   *Saururus cernuus* L.

The lizard's-tail is a common plant of swamps and marshlands. Fleshy underground rhizomes bear upright shoots with heart-shaped leaves. The flowers are borne in dense, spikelike racemes that characteristically droop at the tip, resembling the tail of a lizard. The flowers lack both sepals and petals, the conspicuous parts being the white filaments of the stamens. There is only one species of *Saururus* in North America and an additional species in eastern Asia. May—July. Fla.—Tex., north into Can.

Dutchman's-Pipe Family   Aristolochiaceae

VIRGINIA SNAKEROOT   *Aristolochia serpentaria* L.

An erect shrub growing to a height of 2 feet, Virginia snakeroot produces flowers, each with a tubular calyx curved like a "Dutchman's pipe." The foul-smelling flowers lack petals, but the madder-purple to crimson calyx is attractive. A single flower is borne at the end of each flowering stem. The aromatic roots were formerly used as a remedy for snakebite. April—June. Rich woods, coves, and stream banks. Fla.—Tex., north to Conn. and N.Y.

Fragrant Ladies'-Tresses

Nodding Ladies'-Tresses

Lizard's-Tail

Virginia Snakeroot

47

DUTCHMAN'S-PIPE

Aristolochia macrophylla Lam.

Dutchman's-pipe is a smooth, high-climbing woody vine with large heart-shaped leaves up to 10 inches long. The flowers are often produced so high above ground that they are overlooked. The "pipe" is formed from an inflated tubular calyx that is strongly curved and bears a maroon or brownish appendage at its apex. May−June. Rich woods and stream banks. Ga.−Ala., north to Pa. *Aristolochia tomentosa* has smaller leaves and densely white-hairy leaves and stems.

WILD GINGER

Asarum canadense L.

A low herb with a pair of soft, downy, heart-shaped leaves, this stemless species grows from a rhizome that has a strong gingery smell when bruised. At ground level in the axil of a leaf, a single brownish urn-shaped flower develops. It is easily distinguished from related species by having 12 stamens, an inferior ovary, and a single style with 6 stigma lobes. This species is not recommended for cultivation because of its tendency to spread rapidly. April−May. Often locally abundant in moist shady hollows. Ga.−Ala., north to Can.

HEARTLEAF, WILD GINGER

Hexastylis arifolia (Michx.) Small

This is the most common species of *Hexastylis* in the state and is distinguished by its halberd-shaped leaves and flowers with a vase-shaped calyx, constricted at the neck, with lobes that flare out at the mouth. In early spring the leaves are bright green, becoming dark purplish-brown with age. Both old and new leaves can be seen in the photograph at right. When crushed, the leaves of all species of *Hexastylis* have the odor of ginger. March−May. Common in moist woods. Fla.−La., north to Va.

HARPER'S GINGER

Hexastylis speciosa Harper

This is Alabama's rarest and most beautiful ginger. It has large arrowhead-shaped leaves, 3−9 inches long, that are glossy green becoming darker, but not mottled, with age. The large, goblet-shaped calyx has a flared mouth revealing a rich brown, striped interior. The flower is borne on a thick stalk 1−3 inches long. Originally reported only from Autauga County, Alabama, the present authors have found it in Chilton County in a pocosinlike area in association with *Drosera, Aletris, Lycopodium,* and *Calopogon.* Infrequent even in these two counties. April−June.

Wild Ginger

Dutchman's-Pipe

Heartleaf

Harper's Ginger

SHUTTLEWORTH'S GINGER   *Hexastylis shuttleworthii* (Britt. & Baker) Small

This species has thin, aromatic, heart-shaped leaves mottled green and white, often with a distinct reticulate pattern evident. The urn-shaped calyx is 1−2 inches long and about an inch broad, with lobes that are reflexed, whitened, and firm. The throat is finely hairy and spotted within. May−July. Rich woods, mountains. Ga.−Ala., north to Va.

WILD GINGER   *Hexastylis minor* (Ashe) Blomquist

The leaves of this wild ginger are 1−3 inches long, heart-shaped, and flared above the middle. Each dark green leaf has a light green reticulate pattern along the veins. The calyx is bell-shaped, and the tube is ½−1½ inches long, with 4 strongly spreading lobes up to ½ inch long. The interior of the calyx is lined with distinct ridges. February−April. Ga.−Ala., north to N.C.

Purslane Family   **Portulacaceae**

SPRING BEAUTY   *Claytonia virginica* L.

In Alabama the first signs of spring often appear as early as January with the blossom of spring beauty. The slender stem grows to a height of up to 10 inches from a deep-seated corm and bears a pair of long, narrow, tapering leaves. Each flower has 2 bractlike sepals and 5 petals that are pinkish with darker, rose-colored veins. The flowers close with darkness but will open again the following day. January−April. Common in woods, thickets, fields. Ga.−Tex., north to Can.

SUN-BRIGHT, ROCK PORTULACA   *Talinum teretifolium* Pursh

The name *teretifolium* means leaves round in cross section, a feature that distinguishes this species of *Talinum* from others in the Southeast. It bears a cluster of succulent leaves about 2 inches long, arising from the lower third of the stem. The flowers, having 5 red to rose-purple petals and 10−20 stamens, remain open for only a few hours in bright sunlight. June−September. Rock outcrops. Ga.−Ala., north to Va.

Shuttleworth's Ginger

Wild Ginger

Spring Beauty

Sun-Bright

Pink Family   Caryophyllaceae

GIANT CHICKWEED   *Stellaria pubera* Michx.

The flowers of this chickweed are larger and more attractive than other chickweeds. It is an erect or spreading perennial, 8—16 inches tall. The leaves are elliptic-oblong, up to 3 inches long. The white flowers are ½ inch in diameter with 5 petals so deeply cleft as to appear to be 10. April—June. Rich woods. Fla.—Miss., north to N.J. The common chickweed, *Stellaria media,* is a spreading, prostrate annual with stem pubescence in distinct lines and small white flowers.

SQUARE FLOWER   *Paronychia erecta* (Chapm.) Shin.

An erect perennial with a wiry, pubescent stem, *Paronychia* grows to a height of 2 feet and develops a distinct taproot. The narrow leaves are up to an inch long with thin translucent stipules. The inflorescences are corymbs arranged distinctly in squares. The 3-veined sepals are hooded and have ciliate margins. June—October. Sand dunes and borders of woods. Coastal Plain. Northern Fla.—Miss.

BOUNCING-BET, SOAPWORT   *Saponaria officinalis* L.

This European native has become thoroughly naturalized in the U.S. and is often seen growing along roadsides. The pink or white flowers are over an inch across, with each petal bearing a pointed appendage at the top of the claw. The sap from this plant will lather in water like soap—thus the common name soapwort. May—October. Common, often forming large clumps, particularly in disturbed areas. Throughout eastern North America.

STARRY CAMPION   *Silene stellata* (L.) Ait.

The starry campion is an erect perennial with stiff stems that branch freely, reaching a height of 2—3 feet. The narrow leaves, mostly in whorls of 4, are smooth or slightly rough to the touch. The white petals have a shallow fringe on the ends and are ½ inch or more long. A capsular fruit develops that splits by six teeth at the top. June—September. Ga.—Tex., north to Mass.

Giant Chickweed

Square Flower

Bouncing-Bet

Starry Campion

BLADDER CAMPION   *Silene cucubalus* Wibel

This species is easily distinguished by the thin, inflated calyx that forms a balloonlike structure around the base of the petals and by the deeply cleft white petals that are without crowns. The sepals also have a distinctive reticulate pattern of veins. It grows to a height of 2 feet and has opposite leaves that are 2 inches long. May—August. Native of Europe, widely naturalized in much of eastern North America.

FIRE PINK, CATCHFLY   *Silene virginica* L.

The sticky stems of this native species of *Silene* led to the common name catchfly. The bright red flowers, about 1½—2 inches across, have petals deeply notched at the apex. The opposite leaves are widest toward the ends. Small clumps of fire pink add brightness to the landscape along roadsides and in open woods. April—June. Common. Ga.—Ala. north into Can.

PINK CATCHFLY, WILD PINK   *Silene caroliniana* var. *wherryi* (Small)Fern.

This species also has sticky stems but is readily distinguishable from *Silene virginica* by its white or pink flowers with petals that are only slightly notched. The opposite leaves are clustered toward the base, and the stems tend to be sticky, primarily toward the top. April—June. Ga.—Ala., north to Va. The sleepy catchfly, *S. antirrhina*, is distinctive in having small white flowers and blackish sticky zones on the stem between leaf pairs.

ROUND-LEAVED CATCHFLY   *Silene rotundifolia* Nutt.

This bright scarlet catchfly can be distinguished by its round to ovate leaves. The flowers are borne in the axils of foliage leaves, and the petals are cleft and toothed at the apex. The photo at right was made on a high bluff in Bankhead National Forest on December 28, although the blooming period is usually from early spring to midsummer. Rocky banks, cliffs, ledges. Ga.—Ala., north to Va.

Bladder Campion

Fire Pink

Pink Catchfly

Round-leaved Catchfly

Water Lily Family   Nymphaeaceae

YELLOW POND LILY, SPATTERDOCK   *Nuphar luteum* (L.) Sibthorp & Smith

The large round submersed leaves of spatterdock have a deep sinus at the base of the blade and a stout petiole 6−12 inches long. The small yellow flowers are 1−1½ inches in diameter and have 5−14 showy sepals, the outer ones green, the inner ones mostly yellow or reddish. The numerous petals are attached with the numerous stamens on the receptacle beneath the ovary. April−October. Pond margins and swamps. Throughout eastern U.S.

FRAGRANT WATER LILY   *Nymphaea odorata* Ait.

Nymphaea is a particularly good genus to use in studying flower structure. In these large flowers, it is easy to see a morphological transition from sepals to petals to stamens. The flowers of *N. odorata* are very fragrant, and have numerous white or pinkish petals up to 4 inches long. The numerous stamens are inserted on the ovary, and the outer ones have petallike filaments. June−September. Ponds, sluggish streams, throughout eastern U.S. *Nymphaea mexicana* has yellow petals and smaller flowers; *N. elegans* has blue flowers.

Lotus Family   Nelumbonaceae

AMERICAN LOTUS, POND-NUTS   *Nelumbo lutea* (Willd.) Pers.

There are two species of *Nelumbo*, one native to eastern North America, the other to southeast Asia. The American lotus has yellow flowers 3−10 inches across. The round leaves are very large, 1−2 feet in diameter, and each leaf is held up out of the water by a stout petiole that is attached in the center of the blade. The funnellike seed pod has many indentations in the flat top where the seeds are imbedded. These pods are often collected for dried arrangements. Both the seeds and the underground tubers are edible. June−September. Ponds and sluggish streams throughout eastern U.S. The Asian species, *N. nucifera*, occasionally escapes from cultivation but can be distinguished by its pink petals.

Buttercup Family   Ranunculaceae

COLUMBINE   *Aquilegia canadensis* L.

The unusual flowers of columbine have 5 petals, each of which is formed into a tube with a long spur containing nectaries. The petals are clustered together so that the spurs point upward and the sepals downward. These red and yellow flowers are particularly adapted for pollination by hummingbirds. These small birds can hover at any angle and extract nectar from the long spurs. The delicate leaves are compound, becoming reduced on the upper part of the stem. March−May. Rocky woods and meadows. Fla.−Ala., north into Can.

Yellow Pond Lily

Fragrant Water Lily

Columbine

American Lotus

Dwarf Larkspur

Delphinium tricorne Michx.

The word *Delphinium* is from the Greek for dolphin, alluding to the resemblance of the flower to a dolphin. Each of the purple or dark blue flowers has 5 sepals with one prolonged into a spur. There are 4 petals, 2 with spurs that extend into the sepal spur, and 2 with clawlike stalks at the base. The seeds are black and shining. There is a white-flowered form of this species, and occasionally plants are found with blue flowers variegated with white. March—May. Rich woods, often in calcareous soil. Ga.—Miss., north to Pa.

Tall Larkspur

Delphinium exaltatum Ait.

The stem and the inflorescence of the tall larkspur are slender, straight, erect, and smooth except where the flowers are borne. It grows to a height of over 6 feet, bearing numerous deeply cut leaves. The flowers are blue or white, forming brown seeds without wings. July—September. Rich woods and roadsides. Ga.—Ala., north to Pa. A related species, *Delphinium carolinianum*, has a shorter, hairy stem and scaly winged seeds.

Monkshood

Aconitum uncinatum L.

Monkshood is a weak-stemmed perennial that grows to a height of 5 feet from a tuberous root. The palmate leaves are heart-shaped and deeply divided with 3—5 lobes. The flowers are irregular with the calyx highly modified. Of the 5 sepals, 2 elliptic, 2 are spatulate, and the uppermost one is shaped like a helmet or hood. The petals are very small, with 2 enclosed under the hood. Both the seeds and the tubers contain poisonous alkaloids. August—October. Rich woods. Ga.—Ala., north to Pa.

Buttercup

Ranunculus sardous Crantz

A shallow-rooted annual, *Ranunculus sardous* is a native of Europe that has become widespread over Alabama in disturbed areas. It is a showy plant with erect stems bearing numerous flowers. The leaves are compound, each usually with 3 leaflets that are also lobed or cleft. The flowers are about an inch across, with reflexed sepals and golden-yellow petals. The fruits have recurved beaks and numerous small projections on the surface. April—June. Low fields and disturbed areas. Ga.—Ala., north to N.Y. and Pa. This species is very similar to the bulbous buttercup, *R. bulbosa*, which can be readily distinguished by its bulbous base.

Tall Larkspur

Dwarf Larkspur

Monkshood

Buttercup

59

YELLOWROOT   *Xanthorhiza simplicissima* Marsh.

This is an unusual member of the buttercup family because it is a woody shrub. It grows to a height of about 2 feet and has pinnately divided leaves. Both the stem and the root have bright yellow inner bark and wood. The flowers are purple brown in elongate racemes. The yellow sap was used by primitive man as a dye and as a medicine. April—May. Along shady streams. Ga.—Miss., north to N.Y.

BLACK SNAKEROOT, BUGBANE   *Cimicifuga racemosa* Nutt.

The tallest member of the buttercup family, black snakeroot is a coarse perennial that grows to a height of 7 feet or more from a knotty rhizome. The leaves are divided into 3 segments, and each segment is divided once or twice again into 3 stalked segments. Elongate racemes bear numerous small apetalous flowers with 4 sepals and a single pistil. There is a distinctive row of petallike, sterile stamens, each bearing a single horn. May—June. Rich woods, primarily in the mountains. Ga.—Ala., north into Can. *Cimicifuga americana* is smaller, but the sterile stamens each bear 2 horns and there are 3—8 pistils.

WHITE BANEBERRY, DOLL'S-EYES   *Actaea pachypoda* Ell.

Baneberries are small plants, about 2 feet tall, with leaves that are twice compound into 3-lobed segments. The flowers, borne in loose racemes, have 4—10 small white petals that drop off soon after the flower opens. The single pistil forms a waxy white berry with a single dark spot formed around the stigma, which looks like a "doll's eye." The beautiful white berries are very poisonous if eaten and have caused serious illness and even death. April—May. Damp woods. Ga.—La., north into Can.

VIRGIN'S-BOWER   *Clematis virginiana* L.

Clematis is a very attractive vine, not only during the blooming period but also in autumn when the long persistent styles aid in the dissemination of the seeds. The vinelike stems of virgin's-bower are angled and pubescent, bearing leaves that are divided into 3 leaflets. Cymes of greenish-white apetalous flowers with 4 sepals are borne in the axils of stem leaves. July—September. Low woods, stream banks. Ga.—La., north into Can.

Yellowroot

Black Snakeroot

White Baneberry

Virgin's-Bower

LEATHERFLOWER
Clematis viorna L.

A sprawling vine with angled stems, the leaves of leatherflower are thin, membranaceous, and divided into 3—7 leaflets. The flowers are borne singly and have thick leathery sepals that are reddish-brown, up to an inch long, and recurved at the tips. May—September. Rich woods. Ga.—Tex., north to Pa. Other species with thick sepals include *Clematis crispa*, with sepals that have wavy margins, *C. glaucophylla*, which has a rounded stem, and *C. reticulata*, which has thick leathery leaves with a raised, reticulate venation.

FALSE RUE ANEMONE
Isopyrum biternatum (Raf.) T. & G.

This species is often confused with the rue anemone but can easily be distinguished by a number of characteristics. *Isopyrum* has leaves that are divided into 3 leaflets, with each leaflet deeply 3-lobed. The stems and leaf stalks are green—not black as in the rue anemone. A flower has usually 5 white petallike sepals, numerous stamens with white filaments, and 2—5 widely spreading pistils. March—April. Rich woods, particularly on calcareous slopes. Fla.—Tex., north to Can.

RUE ANEMONE
Thalictrum thalictroides (L.) Boivin

These delicate, early spring perennials grow 4—6 inches high from a cluster of tubers. The black wiry stems bear leaves that are divided into 3 leaflets, and each leaflet is also slightly 3-lobed at the apex. There are 5—8 white petallike sepals, but no true petals. The 4—15 separate pistils, as well as the black stems, serve to distinguish this species from the false rue anemone treated above. March—May. Rich woods and moist, rocky slopes. Fla.—Miss., north to Me.

EARLY MEADOW RUE
Thalictrum dioicum L.

An erect, herbaceous species, the early meadow rue grows to a height of almost 3 feet. The leaves, with 3 leaflets, resemble those of the rue anemone, but the present species is easily distinguished. It has unisexual flowers, with the male and female flowers on separate plants. The stamens are pendulous and have long thin filaments and yellow anthers. March—April. Rich woods. Ga.—Ala., north into Can.

Leatherflower

Rue Anemone

False Rue Anemone

Early Meadow Rue

MEADOW RUE   *Thalictrum polygamum* Muhl.

A large plant, up to 5 feet high, the meadow rue has compound leaves with the leaflets usually 3-lobed. The flowers have no petals and bear either pistils or stamens but not both. The individual plants may bear either male or female flowers or both. The fruits are sessile and smooth. This is a late blooming plant that is difficult to distinguish from *Thalictrum subrotundum*, a species having rounded leaflets and a more lax habit. May—July. Rich woods and meadows. Ga.—Miss., north into Can.

ROUND-LOBED LIVERLEAF, HEPATICA   *Hepatica americana* (DC.) Ker

This lovely perennial herb has a short rhizome from which the characteristic liver-shaped leaves arise. The 3-lobed leaves are green when young, turning reddish-brown variegated with green as they persist into the winter. The lower surface of the leaves is purplish, and the petioles are up to 7 inches long, bearing long silky hairs. The solitary flowers, about an inch across, lack petals but have 5—12 white, pink, or blue sepals that resemble petals. The fruit is a cluster of achenes that are ovoid and hairy. February—April. Rich woods, chiefly on the Piedmont. Ga.—Miss., north into Can.

SHARP-LOBED LIVERLEAF, HEPATICA   *Hepatica acutiloba* DC.

This species of *Hepatica* is very similar to *H. americana*, differing primarily in the shape of the leaves and sepals. The leaves of the sharp-lobed hepatica have lobes that are acute rather than obtuse or rounded. Likewise, the sepals and the involucral bracts at the base of the flower (often confused with sepals) are sharp-pointed in this species. These two species are distributed in the same general area but usually do not occur together. When they do occur together, they often interbreed. February—April. Rich woods, often on calcareous sites. Ga.—Miss., north to Me. and Minn.

WOOD ANEMONE, THIMBLEWEED   *Anemone quinquefolia* L.

An herbaceous perennial, the wood anemone is one of the first flowers to bloom in the spring. There is a single basal leaf and a pair of stem leaves that are usually deeply divided into 3—5 lobes or clefts. The specific name *quinquefolia* refers to the 5 parts of the leaf. The flowers are borne singly and, although they lack petals, the 5—6 sepals are white and resemble petals. A cluster of small, densely hairy fruits is formed shortly after the flowering period. This is a northern species that grows primarily in the mountains and in cool ravines. March—May. Ala.—Tenn., north into Can. A closely related species, *Anemone lancifolia*, is very similar but has lateral leaves that are less deeply cut and usually only 3-lobed.

Meadow Rue

Round-lobed Liverleaf

Sharp-lobed Liverleaf

Wood Anemone

CAROLINA ANEMONE, WINDFLOWER   *Anemone caroliniana* Walt.

This herbaceous species grows to a height of about a foot from a single rounded tuber. The 2—3 basal leaves are usually divided into 3 segments, and the 2—3 opposite or whorled stem leaves bear solitary flowers in their axils. The stems and leaves are covered with long shaggy hairs. Lacking petals, the flowers have 10—20 white sepals that resemble petals. A dense cylindrical cluster of achenes, arranged in a spiral pattern, persists for up to a month after the sepals are shed. March—April. Woods, fields, and prairies. Ga.—Miss., north to N.C.

Magnolia Family   Magnoliaceae

TULIP TREE, YELLOW POPLAR   *Liriodendron tulipifera* L.

This beautiful tree has both leaves and flowers that easily distinguish it from all other species. The broad leaves with a flat or shallowly notched apex are like those of no other tree. The flowers, approximately the same size and shape as tulip flowers, have a greenish-yellow perianth with darker orange markings within. Mature trees may reach a height of up to 150 feet and a diameter of 6—8 feet. April—June. Rich low woods and ravines. Ala.—Tex., north to southern Can. There is a single species of *Liriodendron* in eastern North America and an additional species in eastern Asia.

Illicium Family   Illiciaceae

ANISE BUSH, STAR ANISE   *Illicium floridanum* Ell.

Anise bush is one of the characteristic species of the low swampy woodlands of the Deep South. It is an evergreen shrub with elliptic leaves that are thick and slightly fleshy. When crushed, the leaves have a very strong odor similar to that of anise. The dark crimson flowers have numerous strap-shaped perianth parts and 2 or more cycles of stamens with strap-shaped filaments. The flowers have a fishy odor at maturity. The fruit is composed of a circle of simple pistils fused laterally to form a starlike ring. March—May. Low swamps and stream bottoms. Fla.—La.

Pawpaw Family   Annonaceae

PAWPAW   *Asimina triloba* (L.) Dunal

A slender shrub or small tree, the pawpaw has oblong leaves up to a foot long. The leaves are rusty-hairy beneath and faintly aromatic when crushed. The flowers, appearing just before the leaves, are green at first but turn a rich purple brown at maturity. There are 3 small sepals and 2 cycles of 3 petals. The fruit, about 2 inches long, is fragrant, fleshy, and edible when it ripens in the fall. March—May. Rich woods. Fla.—Tex., north to N.Y. and southern Ont. The dwarf pawpaw, *Asimina parviflora*, is a small shrub of drier sites and has smaller flowers and fruits.

Carolina Anemone

Tulip Tree

Anise Bush

Pawpaw

Calycanthus Family

Calycanthaceae

SWEET-SHRUB

Calycanthus floridus L.

This aromatic shrub has opposite leaves with smooth margins and grows to a height of 5—10 feet. The flowers are borne on the ends of branches and have numerous dark red or maroon perianth parts that are not differentiated into sepals and petals. Numerous stamens and simple pistils are enclosed within the perianth. The flowers have a strong fruity fragrance similar to that of strawberries. April—May. Rich woods. Fla.—Miss., north to Va. and W. Va.

Barberry Family

Berberidaceae

TWINLEAF, RHEUMATISM-ROOT

Jeffersonia diphylla (L.) Pers.

Twinleaf is a glabrous woodland perennial herb that grows from a rhizome to a height of 5—8 inches by the time of flowering but continues to elongate to a height of about 18 inches. The kidney-shaped leaves are deeply parted into 2 smooth-margined leaflets. Borne singly on naked stems, the white flowers each have 4 petallike sepals and 8 petals. The capsules are leathery and open by a transverse slit. The generic name was given in honor of Thomas Jefferson. March—April. Rich, moist woods usually on calcareous sites. Rare in Alabama. Ala., north to N. Y. and Wis.

MAY APPLE, MANDRAKE

Podophyllum peltatum L.

May apple is a smooth perennial herb, 8—20 inches tall, with an elongate underground rhizome that spreads to form colonies. At the top of the stem is a pair of rounded leaves, each of which is palmately divided into 5—9 segments. Young plants often have only one leaf, but these do not produce flowers. A single nodding waxy-white flower, 1—2 inches across, appears in early spring beneath the leaves at the top of the stem. There are 6—9 petals and 12—18 stamens. The fruit is a fleshy, yellowish-green or reddish berry, 1—2 inches long, and is edible. The roots, stems, and leaves, however, are poisonous if eaten. Late March—May. Mixed deciduous forests, alluvial woodlands and meadows. Fla.—Tex., north into Can.

Moonseed Family

Menispermaceae

CAROLINA MOONSEED, CORALBEADS

Cocculus carolinus (L.) DC.

A beautiful vine climbing over fences, rocks, and trees, Carolina moonseed has heart-shaped leaves that are smooth above and finely hairy beneath. The flowers are unisexual, with only the male flowers or the female flowers present on a single plant. Borne in terminal or axillary panicles, the flowers have perianth segments that are poorly differentiated into sepals and petals. The fruit is a red drupe about ¼ inch in diameter containing a single coiled seed. June—August. Sandy woods and fields. Fla.—Tex., north to Va. and Ky.

Sweet-Shrub

Twinleaf

May Apple

Carolina Moonseed

Poppy Family   Papaveraceae

BLOODROOT   *Sanguinaria canadensis* L.

A stemless perennial 4—12 inches tall, bloodroot is a true harbinger of spring. The leaf, usually one per plant, is somewhat kidney-shaped and irregularly palmately lobed or parted. Borne on a leafless stalk, the solitary flower has 2 sepals that enclose the flower bud and fall soon after the flower opens. The 8—12 petals are about an inch long and they, too, are soon shed. The rhizome, flowering stalk, and leaves contain a reddish juice that was used by Indians for body paint and as a red dye. The rhizomes are purported to be poisonous if eaten. March—April. Mixed deciduous forests, chiefly mountains and Piedmont, becoming rare in Alabama. Fla.—Tex., north into Can.

WHITE PRICKLY POPPY   *Argemone albiflora* Hornem.

The prickly poppy is an annual herb 1—3 feet tall with thistlelike foliage containing a white or clear latex. The sessile leaves are irregularly cleft into numerous leaflets with spiny-toothed margins. The large showy flowers, terminating the branches, have 2—3 sepals and 4—6 petals. The capsules are spiny and shed their seeds through 3—6 valvelike openings at the top. April—May. Roadsides and waste places. Fla.—Tex. and Mo., west and north to Cal. and Ida. The yellow prickly poppy, *Papaver mexicana*, is similar but has yellow flowers. The opium poppy, *P. somniferum*, is rarely found outside of cultivation.

Fumitory Family   Fumariaceae

DUTCHMAN'S-BREECHES   *Dicentra cucullaria* (L.) Bernh.

This delicate perennial herb grows from a short bulblet-bearing rootstock. The leaves are divided into 3 leaflets with each of these further divided into numerous segments that are almost linear. The flowers are white, sometimes tinged with pink, and are borne in racemes that overtop the leaves. The common name is derived from the fancied resemblance of the 2-spurred corolla to a pair of miniature pantaloons about ½ inch long. March—April. Rich woods, north-facing slopes and river banks. Mountains and Piedmont. Fla.—Ala., north into Can. A closely related species, *Dicentra canadensis*, commonly known as squirrel-corn, has larger leaves, and corolla spurs that are more rounded and less divergent.

WILD FUMEWORT, CORYDALIS   *Corydalis micrantha* (Engelm.) Gray

An erect or somewhat reclining annual 4—16 inches tall, fumewort has pinnately compound leaves with the leaflets further divided into numerous linear segments. Elevated above the leaves are racemes of clear yellow flowers. The corolla is similar to that of *Dicentra* but differs in having only one spurred petal, the spur being about ½ inch long. The roots have a pungent odor when bruised. March—April. Sandy soil, Coastal Plain. Fla.—Tex., north to Va. and Mo. A related species, *Corydalis flavula*, chiefly of alluvial woods, differs in having a shorter spur, usually only about ⅛ inch long, and seeds with a narrow marginal ring.

Bloodroot

White Prickly Poppy

Dutchman's-Breeches

Wild Fumewort

Mustard Family Brassicaceae

TWO-LEAVED TOOTHWORT, CRINKLEROOT   *Cardamine diphylla* (Michx.) Wood

An herbaceous perennial, this toothwort grows to a height of 8—16 inches from a long continuous rhizome that is thickened at the nodes but not segmented. The leaves are deeply dissected and appear to be compound. The basal leaves, when present, arise from a rhizome. Both the Latin name and the common name refer to the pair of opposite stem leaves. The flowers, borne in a short terminal raceme, have each 4 sepals, 4 petals, and 6 stamens. As is characteristic of the family, 4 of the 6 stamens are longer than the others. April—May. Chiefly in the mountains and Piedmont. Ala. north into Can. A related species, *Cardamine angustata*, differs in having a segmented rhizome.

CUT-LEAVED TOOTHWORT, THREE-LEAVED TOOTHWORT   *Cardamine concatenata* (Michx.) Ahles

This species closely resembles *Cardamine diphylla*, but differs not only in having a distinctive rhizome that is white and jointed but also in having three stem leaves in a whorl. Each stem leaf is cleft into 3—5 divisions and each division is further lobed or deeply toothed. The basal leaves, if present, are similar to the stem leaves. The flowers are like those of *C. diphylla*, but the petals are sometimes pink. March—May. Alluvial woods and slopes. Fla.—La., north into Can.

WAREA   *Warea cuneifolia* (Muhl.) Nutt.

Warea is a slender, smooth annual with erect stems up to 4 feet tall, usually branching freely. The leaves are about an inch long, not lobed or divided, and taper to a wedgelike base. Borne in headlike racemes terminating the branches, the flowers have 4 pink to whitish petals that narrow to a clawlike base. The sickle-shaped pods are about 2 inches long. July—September. Dry sandhills, Coastal Plain. Fla.—Ala., north to S. C. A related species, found primarily in Florida but also in extreme south Alabama, is *W. sessilifolia*, easily distinguished by its smaller leaves that are oval with a rounded, nearly sessile base.

Pitcher Plant Family Sarraceniaceae

PITCHER PLANT, SIDESADDLE PLANT   *Sarracenia purpurea* L.

This pitcher plant is a perennial bog plant, up to a foot tall, with hollow pitcherlike leaves. The evergreen leaves, widest near the middle, have hoods that arch above but do not cover the mouths of the pitchers. Because of numerous downward pointing hairs lining the inside of the lip of the pitcher, insects are guided into the mouth of the trap. The nodding flowers are about 2 inches across with 5 maroon petals and 5 greenish, persistent sepals. Numerous stamens are partially hidden from view by the short style that is expanded at the summit into an umbrella-shaped stigma. April—May. Sphagnum bogs and moist savannas, chiefly on the Coastal Plain. Fla.—La., north into Can.

Two-leaved Toothwort

Cut-leaved Toothwort

Warea

Pitcher Plant

YELLOW PITCHER PLANT, TRUMPETS   *Sarracenia flava* L.

This pitcher plant is readily distinguishable by its erect, trumpet-shaped, yellowish-green, leaves that are 12—40 inches high and are conspicuously veined and narrowly winged. The hood arches over, but does not closely cover the mouth of the pitcher. Solitary and nodding, the flowers, 4—5 inches in diameter, have 5 bright yellow drooping petals and a strong musty odor. March—May. Wet pinelands and bogs. La.—Fla., north to Va.

WINGED PITCHER PLANT, YELLOW TRUMPETS   *Sarracenia alata* (Wood) Wood

Very similar to the yellow pitcher plant, the winged pitcher plant can be distinguished by its narrower pitchers that are widely winged for the full length of the leaf. The flowers are also distinctive, being greenish-yellow rather than bright yellow. May—June. Damp pineland. Ala.—Tex.

CRIMSON PITCHER PLANT, FIDDLER'S-TRUMPET   *Sarracenia leucophylla* Raf.

The leaves of this plant are 1—4 feet tall, erect, and trumpet-shaped. The trumpets are only slightly winged, but sometimes the tube fails to develop and the entire leaf is flat and winglike. The leaves are green at base, shading to white with a network of reddish-purple veins in the upper portion. The hood is erect and rounded with a distinctly wavy and recurved margin. The flowers are 2—3 inches broad and solitary on an erect stem that is often as tall as the leaves. The crimson or reddish-purple petals are fiddle-shaped. April. Sandy bogs along the Coastal Plain. Fla.—Ga., west to Miss.

PARROT PITCHER PLANT, PARROT-BEAKS   *Sarracenia psittacina* Michx.

Smallest of the Alabama pitcher plants, the parrot pitcher plant has a basal rosette of evergreen leaves that are only 2—6 inches long. Each pitcher has a broad, obovate wing, is spotted with white, and has conspicuous reddish-purple veins, particularly on the upper part of the leaf. Strongly incurved, the hood almost closes the mouth of the pitcher and thereby causes the leaf to bear some resemblance to a parrot's beak. The dark reddish-purple flowers are about 2 inches across and are borne singly on erect leafless stems about a foot tall. April—May. Lowlands along the Coastal Plain. Fla.—La.

Yellow Pitcher Plant

Winged Pitcher Plant

Crimson Pitcher Plant

Parrot Pitcher Plant

MOUNTAIN PITCHER PLANT   *Sarracenia oreophila* Wherry

The mountain pitcher plant is very similar to *Sarracenia flava*, having erect, hollow, trumpet-shaped leaves that are winged and have yellow-green veins. It is easily distinguished, however, by the leaf clusters that contain a number of short, flat, basal leaves as well as the erect trumpets. The flowers are borne singly on bare stems and have distinctly small petals, not much larger than the sepals. May—June. Damp ditches, stream banks in the mountains. Northeastern Ala.—Ga.

Sundew Family   Droseraceae

SUNDEW   *Drosera intermedia* Hayne

The sundews are insectivorous plants with leaves that bear glandular hairs that secrete a glistening, sticky fluid. Small insects and spiders become caught in the fluid and are subsequently digested by enzymes secreted by the plant. The leaves of *Drosera intermedia* have blades that are narrowly spatula-shaped with long petioles. Borne in a one-sided raceme, nodding at the apex and strongly curved toward the base, the flowers are white or pinkish, and form seeds that are black and warty. July—September. Bogs, savannas, and wet ditches, often in standing water. Fla.—Tex., north into Can. *Drosera rotundifolia* has leaf blades broader than long, abruptly narrowed into a slender petiole. *Drosera leucantha* has wedge-shaped leaf blades on short, flat petioles. The stem is only 1—4 inches tall, bearing flowers more than ½ inch across.

DEW-THREADS, THREAD-LEAF SUNDEW   *Drosera filiformis* Raf.

Bearing numerous gland-tipped hairs, the filamentous leaves of this species are about a foot tall. The expanded petiole bases end in a cormlike structure from which the leafless flowering stem arises. The rose-purple flowers produce seeds that are black with a netlike pattern of ridges. June. Savannas, low pinelands, and wet sandy roadsides. Coastal Plain. Fla.—La., north to S. C.

Saxifrage Family   Saxifragaceae

FOAMFLOWER, FALSE MITERWORT   *Tiarella cordifolia* L.

One of the most attractive spring wildflowers in the woods of Alabama, the foamflower has a basal rosette of leaves shaped like maple leaves, with the upper and lower surfaces rough and hairy. The white flowers are borne in a feathery raceme terminating a naked stem that grows to a height of about one foot. The small flowers are about ¼ inch across with 5 clawed petals. 10 protruding stamens tipped with orange anthers, and a single 2-lobed pistil in the center. The seed capsule is partially divided into two unequal parts somewhat resembling a tiara, from which the name *Tiarella* was derived. March—June. Rich woods, primarily mountains and Plateau. Ga.—Ala., north into Can. Of the two distinct varieties of this species, var. *cordifolia* has underground stolons, and var. *collina* lacks such stolons.

Mountain Pitcher Plant

Sundew

Dew-Threads

Foamflower

ALUMROOT
Heuchera americana L.

As alumroots and foamflowers are very similar and often grow in the same area, they are easily confused. The more rounded leaf of alumroot is irregularly but not deeply lobed, and is hairy on the veins of the underside. Alumroot has a branching, compound inflorescence consisting of clusters of racemes, in contrast to the simple raceme of foamflower. Also, the small flowers of alumroot have pink to lavender petals and only 5 protruding stamens. The fruit is a capsule with dark red spiny seeds. April—June. Chiefly mountains and Piedmont. Ala.—Ga., north into Can.

GRASS-OF-PARNASSUS
Parnassia asarifolia Vent.

The common name of this species is very misleading, as this plant is not a grass. The name was derived from a name given by the Greek physician Dioscorides to a similar species that supposedly grew on Mount Parnassus. The basal leaves of *Parnassia asarifolia* are kidney-shaped, and the single stem leaf is small, clasping, and usually heart-shaped. The flowers have 5 creamy-white petals that are longitudinally striped with 11—15 green veins, and clawed near the base. There are 5 sepals, 5 fertile stamens, and 5 sterile stamens circling the green pistil. August—October. Springs, bogs, and wet slopes. Ga.—Ala., north to Va., W. Va. Also growing in Alabama, two related species have petals that are not clawed; *P. grandiflora* has leaves longer than wide and petals with 7—9 main veins; *P. caroliniana* has ovate basal leaves and 9—19 main veins.

EARLY SAXIFRAGE
Saxifraga virginiensis Michx.

This is the most common saxifrage in the state and one of the first wildflowers to bloom each spring. The ovate to elliptic leaves form a basal rosette around a flowering stem that is downy, 12—18 inches tall, and terminated by a cyme of white flowers. Just over ¼ inch across, each small flower has 5 sepals, 5 petals, 10 stamens with golden anthers, and a pistil deeply divided into two parts that form two separate seed pods. March—May. Rock outcrops and gravelly soils. Ga.—Miss., north into Can.

OAK-LEAF HYDRANGEA, SEVEN-BARK
Hydrangea quercifolia Bartr.

This native shrub is attractive during every season of the year. When cultivated in sunny areas, it forms a fairly dense shrub, but in its natural habitat in moist, shady woodlands, it is usually open, with lax, ascending branches. The leaves are 6—8 inches long and coarsely lobed. The flower clusters are up to a foot long and contain small fertile flowers and much larger sterile flowers, the latter having 4 white petallike sepals that later turn pinkish and finally brown, and persist on the plant into winter. April—June. Northern Fla.—Miss., north to Tenn. and Ga. *Hydrangea arborescens* has ovate leaves and smaller, flat-topped flower clusters.

Alumroot

Grass-of-Parnassus

Early Saxifrage

Oak-Leaf Hydrangea

Rose Family   **Rosaceae**

SNOW WREATH   *Neviusia alabamensis* Gray

This rare shrub, once thought to be endemic to Alabama, was discovered along the Black Warrior River near Tuscaloosa in 1857 by Rev. R. D. Nevius and Professor W. S. Wyman. Growing 3−8 feet tall, snow wreath has simple, ovate, bright green leaves with doubly toothed margins and smooth surfaces. Showy, greenish-white, odorless flowers are borne in leafy cymes. Each flower is composed of 5 pointed sepals, numerous stamens with long filaments, but no petals. Spreading vegetatively by root sprouts, the plants are easily transplanted into cultivation. March−April. Rich, damp soils on river bluffs, very narrowly distributed in two areas, one in Alabama, the other in Ark. and Mo.

CINQUEFOIL, FIVE-FINGERS   *Potentilla canadensis* L.

This plant has a creeping stem and shiny, dark green leaves that are palmately compound with 5 leaflets. The single flower stalk is borne in the axil of the first fully developed leaf (with 5 leaflets). About ½ inch wide, each flower has 5 petals, numerous stamens, and numerous simple pistils. The name *Potentilla* means little powerful one, alluding to its alleged strength in medicinal preparations. March−May. Open woods, pastures, and fields. Ga.−Ala., north into Can. A very similar species, *P. simplex*, is usually more upright in habit and has the flowering stalk borne in the axil of the second mature leaf.

ROUGH CINQUEFOIL   *Potentilla recta* L.

Native to Europe but now spreading rapidly over eastern North America, rough cinquefoil is a perennial plant bearing several ascending or erect, hairy stems that grow to a height of about 2 feet from a single crown. The leaves are palmately compound with 5−7, or rarely, 9 leaflets. At the base of the leaves is a conspicuous comblike stipule. Borne in compound cymes, the flowers are about an inch across and have pale yellow petals that are notched at the apex and numerous stamens and simple pistils. April−July. Meadows, pastures, and waste places. Ga., Ala., Tenn., north into Can.

CHICKASAW ROSE, MACARTNEY ROSE   *Rosa bracteata* Wendl.

A native of Asia, this rose has now become widespread in the South and in some areas is a serious pest. Difficult to control, it forms dense clumps several feet across in pastures. The semievergreen leaves are pinnately compound, usually with 5−9 leaflets. The flowers are about 2 inches across, with white petals and numerous yellow stamens. April−May, and intermittently throughout the summer and early fall. Ga.−Miss., north to Va. The similar Cherokee rose, *Rosa laevigata*, can be distinguished by having leaves with only 3 leaflets on the flowering branches.

Snow Wreath

Cinquefoil

Rough Cinquefoil

Chickasaw Rose

GOAT'S-BEARD   *Aruncus dioicus* (Walt.) Fern.

As the name *dioicus* indicates, goat's-beard is dioecious, with the male and female flowers on separate plants. Growing to a height of 7—10 feet from a large rootstock, this species has compound leaves, the lower ones sometimes 2—3 times compound with the segments narrow, pointed, and toothed. The leaves of goat's-beard lack stipules. Both male and female flowers are white and borne in elongate, compound racemes. The male flowers, having numerous stamens, are more showy than the female flowers that have 3 pistils and small nonfunctional anthers. The fruit is a pod that splits along one side. May—June. Rich moist woods, mountains and Piedmont. Ga.—Ala., north to N. Y.

BOWMAN'S-ROOT, AMERICAN IPECAC   *Gillenia trifoliata* (L.) Moench

Bowman's-root grows to a height of about 3 feet, bearing compound leaves divided into 3 sessile leaflets. At the base of each leaf 2 small stipules, about ¼ inch long, appear to be an additional pair of much-reduced leaflets. Ragged in appearance due to the irregular size and habit of the petals, the flowers have numerous stamens and 5 separate pistils that mature into small pods that split along one side. April—June. Woods. Ga.—Ala., north into Can. *Gillenia stipulata* is similar but has much larger, fluted stipules up to an inch long.

Bean Family   Fabaceae

SENSITIVE BRIER   *Schrankia microphylla* (Solander ex Smith) Macbr.

This perennial vinelike herb is sparingly prickly, with prostrate to weakly arching stems. The leaves are twice pinnately compound and the small leaflets are sensitive to touch, slowly closing when either touched or jarred. Bright pink or rose purple, the many 5-lobed tubular flowers form globular clusters almost an inch in diameter. Protruding from the flowers, the numerous stamens with their red filaments and yellow anthers make these small balls conspicuous. The seed pods are 3—6 inches long, sparingly prickly. June—September. Dry woods, pinelands, fields. Fla.—Tex., north to Va. and Ky. Cat-Claw, *Schrankia nuttallii*, is similar but can be distinguished by having hooked prickles and 4—6 pairs of leaflets.

PARTRIDGE PEA   *Cassia fasciculata* Michx.

An herbaceous annual, 1—3 feet tall, partridge pea has pinnately compound leaves. The 6—15 pairs of leaflets are less than an inch long and sensitive to touch. There is a conspicuous saucer-shaped gland near the middle of the petiole. An inch or more across, the bright yellow flowers have 5 irregularly-sized petals, 2—3 often with a purple spot at the base. There are 10 stamens, 4 with yellow anthers and 6 with purple anthers. June—September. Old fields, roadsides, and disturbed areas. Fla.—Tex., north to Mass. and Minn. Sicklepod, *Cassia obtusifolia*, has strongly curved, sickle-shaped fruits; wild senna, *C. marilandica*, has a thick pod divided into many segments and 3—6 pairs of leaf segments up to 3 inches long.

Goat's-Beard

Bowman's-Root

Sensitive Brier

Partridge Pea

WILD INDIGO, RATTLEWEED

Baptisia tinctoria (L.) R. Br.

A bushy, much-branched plant 2—3½ feet tall, wild indigo has smooth, erect stems and leaves divided into 3 leaflets that are gray-green at maturity, turning black when dry. The leaflets are 1—1½ inches long with a blunt apex and a tapering base. In many loose racemes at the ends of branches are yellow flowers about ½ inch long. The short seed pods are rounded and long-beaked. April—August. Dry woods, clearings, roadsides. Fla—La., north to Me. and Ont.

WHITE FALSE INDIGO, PRAIRIE FALSE INDIGO

Baptisia leucantha T. & G.

Growing up to 5 feet tall, this species has a stout stem with a whitish, powdery covering. The leaves have 3 oblong, blunt leaflets about 2 inches long and small pointed stipules that are quickly shed. Borne in stout racemes 2 inches long, the flowers have white petals with the large standard petal marked with purple. The fruit is a long, drooping legume with a distinct beak. May—July. Open woods, prairies. Ala.—Tex., north to Ohio and Minn.

RATTLEBOX

Crotalaria spectabilis Roth.

An erect annual reaching a height of 3 feet or more, this species has smooth, dark purplish stems that are covered with a whitish powdery film. The freely branching stem bears simple leaves, 5—6 inches long, that are wedge-shaped at the base, broadening toward the middle, and rounded at the apex. Clustered near the top of the plant are many-flowered racemes of bright yellow flowers. The central raceme is up to a foot long. The name *Crotalaria* is derived from a Greek word meaning rattle, referring to the manner in which the loose seeds rattle in the dry, inflated pods. July—October. Fields and waste places. Fla.—Miss., north to Va. A related species, *C. angulata,* is a perennial with trailing stems and only 2—5 flowers in each raceme.

LADY-LUPINE

Lupinus villosus Willd.

This lupine is a showy plant, 1—2 feet high, with several prostrate or erect stems radiating from a woody taproot. Both the stems and leaves are densely covered with long shaggy hairs. The simple, gray-green leaves are elliptic or lanceolate and 2—6 inches long. The flowers vary from pink to lilac to purple, with a reddish-purple spot in the center of the standard petal. March—April. Dry pinelands, sandy barrens, Coastal Plain. Fla.—La., north to N.C. *Lupinus diffusus* is similar but has blue flowers and is covered with short hairs. *Lupinus nuttallii,* also occurring on the outer Coastal Plain, has blue flowers and compound leaves.

Wild Indigo

Rattlebox

White False Indigo

Lady-Lupine

CRIMSON CLOVER   *Trifolium incarnatum* L.

An annual with downy stems up to 2 feet tall and leaves palmately divided into 3 leaflets, crimson clover is easily identified by its deep red flower heads. The flowers are about ½ inch long, and are clustered into dense cylindric racemes, 1–3 inches long. April–June. Fields, roadsides, waste places. Ala.–Miss., north to Va. The red clover, *Trifolium pratense*, is a perennial with narrower leaves and globose flowering heads with pinkish flowers.

RABBIT-FOOT CLOVER   *Trifolium arvense* L.

This clover is an annual with erect, softly downy stems that are 4–12 inches high, and narrow leaflets that are minutely 3-toothed at the tips. Hidden by long, persistent sepals that are covered with dense, plumose hairs, the tiny flowers have white, pink, or red petals. The cylindrical flower clusters appear furlike and are readily distinguished from those of other clovers. April–August. Old fields, waste places. Native to Eurasia, this species has escaped from cultivation and is now widespread over much of North America. *Trifolium repens* is the common white clover of lawns; *T. dubium* is a small trailing yellow-flowered clover of fields and roadsides; and *T. resupinatum* is distinctive in having inverted flowers and inflated fruit clusters.

FALSE INDIGO, INDIGO BUSH   *Amorpha fruticosa* L.

False Indigo is a shrub 6–12 feet tall and bears pinnately compound leaves marked with resinous dots. Borne in clusters of dense racemes, the flowers have but one petal each. Surrounding the stamens and the style, the single standard petal is violet to purple. The 10 stamens have bright yellow anthers, and filaments that are fused basally into a single group. The fruit is a small pod, less than ½ inch long, covered with resinous spots. The name *Amorpha* is from a Greek word meaning without form, in reference to the missing petals. May–June. Stream banks, open woods, and thickets. Fla.–La., north to Pa. and W. Va.

CHEROKEE BEAN, CARDINAL SPEAR   *Erythrina herbacea* L.

An erect, showy plant 2–5 feet tall, the Cherokee bean has prickly branchlets. The leaves are divided into 3 triangular leaflets, 2–4 inches long. Occasionally the leaflets are prickly beneath. Borne in many-flowered, leafless spikes up to 15 inches long, the bright red flowers have greatly reduced petals except for a long back petal (standard) up to 2 inches long. The seed pods are curved, and contain scarlet seeds that are reputed to be poisonous. May–July. Pinelands, thickets, and open woods, Coastal Plain. Ga.–Miss.

Crimson Clover

Rabbit-Foot Clover

False Indigo

Cherokee Bean

GOAT'S-RUE, HOARY PEA   *Tephrosia virginiana* (L.) Pers.

Growing to a height of 1—2 feet, this erect perennial is covered with long, silky, white hairs. Pinnately compound, the leaves have 15-25 paired leaflets and a single terminal leaflet. The flowers are borne in densely flowered, terminal racemes. The individual flowers are about ¾ inch long and bicolored; the large standard petals are cream colored, and the other petals are pink or lavender. May—June. Sandy soil, dry open woods, and roadsides. Fla.—Tex., north into Can.

AMERICAN WISTERIA   *Wisteria frutescens* (L.) Poir.

American wisteria is a woody vine with pinnately compound leaves. There are 9—15 pairs of leaflets and a single terminal leaflet, each leaflet being 1—2½ inches long. Borne in compact racemes 2—6 inches long, the flowers are bluish-purple. The flower stalks and often the sepals bear small club-shaped glands. The smooth fruits are 2—4 inches long. April—May. Moist woods, stream banks, and swamps, chiefly Coastal Plain. Ga.—Ala., north to Va. The Chinese wisteria, *Wisteria sinensis*, has pubescent fruits, lacks the club-shaped glands, and has 7—13 leaflets on each leaf; the Japanese wisteria, *W. floribunda*, is similar to *W. sinensis* but has 13—19 leaflets.

BLACK LOCUST   *Robinia pseudo-acacia* L.

A thick-barked tree, growing to a height of 75 feet, the black locust has pinnately compound leaves that are up to a foot long and divided into 3—10 pairs of ovate to elliptic leaflets. Spinelike stipules often persist at the base of the leaves. The white flowers are borne in drooping racemes 5—10 inches long. Woods and thickets. Ga.—La., north to Pa. and Iowa. Common along roadsides, *Robinia hispida* is easily distinguished by bristly stems and purple or reddish flowers.

GROUNDNUT   *Apios americana* Medic.

This is a twining vine with an underground stem bearing numerous small fleshy tubers that are edible. The leaves are pinnately divided into 5—7 broad, sharply pointed leaflets 1—3 inches long. The fragrant flowers, white on the outside and brownish-red to purple on the inside, are borne in short, densely clustered racemes with distinctly swollen joints at the points at which flowers emerge. The linear beans, two-to-many seeded, open by 2 spirally twisting valves. June—August. Moist woods, thickets, river and creek banks. Ga.—La., north to Can.

Goat's-Rue

American Wisteria

Black Locust

Groundnut

89

BUTTERFLY PEA   *Clitoria mariana* L.

This plant is a twining or trailing, sometimes erect, perennial vine growing 1—4 feet long. The leaves are divided into 3 leaflets 1—3 inches long with the terminal leaflet stalked and with each leaflet bearing at its base a stipulelike appendage. In the showy bluish-lavender flowers, the standard petal is nearly 2 inches wide, conspicuously larger than the other petals. Long and flat, the pods are similar to those of the garden pea and have sticky seeds. June—August. Dry open woods, thickets, roadsides. Fla.—Tex., north to N. Y. and Ill.

SPURRED BUTTERFLY PEA   *Centrosema virginianum* (L.) Benth.

This perennial vine has trailing or climbing stems that reach a length of 3—4 feet. The leaves are divided into 3 leaflets that are highly variable in shape, ranging from linear to ovate. The flowers are blue to violet and have a standard petal 1—1½ inches wide with a conspicuous spur on the back side near the base. The slender pods are 2—4 inches long. The name *Centrosema* refers to the spur on the back of the standard petal that serves to distinguish this plant from *Clitoria.* June—August. Dry, sandy woods and fields. Fla.—Tex., north to N. J.

REDBUD, JUDAS TREE   *Cercis canadensis* L.

A shrub or small tree that may reach a height of 25—30 feet, the redbud has pink to violet flowers that provide one of the brightest displays of spring. Appearing before the leaves, the flowers are borne all over the tree, including the surface of the larger branches. The leaves are heart-shaped, 2—3 inches long, and unlike the leaves of any other plant in the bean family. The fruit is a flat pod, 1—3 inches long. Late February—April. Rich woods, and cut-over areas, particularly in alkaline soil. Fla.—Tex., north to Conn. and Pa.

Wood Sorrel Family   Oxalidaceae

WOOD SORREL, VIOLET SOUR-GRASS   *Oxalis violacea* L.

Wood sorrel is a perennial with leaves and flowers growing to a height of 4—8 inches from a scaly, bulbous base. The leaves are palmately divided into 3 segments, each shaped like an inverted heart; they are green above and reddish or purple beneath. Growing in clusters on a slender flowering stalk, the flowers are about an inch across and have rosy-purple or violet petals. Each sepal has an orange gland at the apex. The name *Oxalis* comes from a Greek word meaning sharp, referring to the sharp or sour taste of the leaves that contain large quantities of calcium oxalate. April—May. Dry upland woods, rocky slopes, shaded banks. Fla.—Tex., north to Mass., S.Dak., and Cal.

Butterfly Pea

Spurred Butterfly Pea

Wood Sorrel

Redbud

LARGE YELLOW WOOD SORREL   *Oxalis grandis* Small

The largest of the yellow-flowered species of *Oxalis*, this erect, sometimes sparingly branched plant grows 1−2 feet tall. The leaves are compound with each of the three leaflets 1−2 inches wide and edged with purple. Borne in clusters slightly above the leaves, the flowers are 1−1½ inches across. The small capsules are downy. May−June. Woods, shaded slopes. Ga.−Ala., north to Pa. and Ill.

Geranium Family   Geraniaceae

WILD GERANIUM, CRANESBILL   *Geranium maculatum* L.

A common and familiar woodland wildflower, wild geranium is an erect perennial, growing 1−2 feet tall from a stout underground rhizome. The leaves are palmately cleft or dissected into 3−7 segments. Borne in loose cymes above the leaves, the flowers are 1−1½ inches across and have rose-purple petals. The mature fruit splits into 5 segments. The 5 styles remain attached at the apex, but coil upward from the base, opening the capsule. The name *Geranium* comes from a Greek word meaning crane, referring to the resemblance of the fruit to a crane's beak. April−May. Woods and meadows. Ga.−Ala., north to Kans. and Me. *Geranium carolinianum* is a weedy species in fields and roadsides, with small pale pink flowers, less than ½ inch across.

Milkwort Family   Polygalaceae

CURTISS' MILKWORT   *Polygala curtissii* Gray

This slender, erect annual has a single stem, 4−12 inches high, sometimes branching above the base, and thick, narrow leaves that are ½−¾ inch long. About ¼ inch across with a rose-purple perianth, the tiny, winged flowers are borne in a dense, headlike raceme. The dense flower cluster is similar to that of clover. According to superstition, cows will increase milk production if they eat certain of the polygalas—thus the common name milkwort. June−October. Open woods and pinelands, Coastal Plain. Ga.−La., north to Del.

YELLOW MILKWORT   *Polygala cymosa* Walt.

Yellow milkwort is a biennial, requiring two years to complete a full cycle from seeds to flowers. The plants are 1−4 feet tall with a basal rosette of lanceolate leaves that are 2−3 inches long. Borne on the stem are smaller linear leaves that become greatly reduced above. Much branched, the terminal portion of the stem bears many dense clusters of yellow flowers. May−July. Wet pinelands, marshes, and meadows, Coastal Plain. Fla.−Tex., north to Del. A smaller species, *Polygala ramosa*, is similar but has spatulate basal leaves.

Large Yellow Wood Sorrel

Wild Geranium

Curtiss' Milkwort

Yellow Milkwort

YELLOW MILKWORT, YELLOW BACHELOR'S-BUTTON   *Polygala lutea* L.

Yellow milkwort is also a biennial with one or several stems rising from a basal rosette of blunt, spatulate leaves. Growing 10—20 inches tall, the stems are simple or occasionally branched and have stem leaves that are small and linear. Borne in dense heads, the flowers vary in color from orange to yellow. Only a few flowering heads are borne on each plant. April—October. Low pinelands, sandy swamps and bogs, Coastal Plain. Fla.—La., north to Pa. and N. Y.

LOW BACHELOR'S-BUTTON   *Polygala nana* (Michx.) DC.

This plant, only 2—6 inches tall, has leaves and flower stems that branch out from the base, giving the entire plant the appearance of a rosette. The basal leaves are broadly spatulate. Usually leafless, the stems bear dense rounded heads of lemon yellow flowers. March—October, sporadically through the winter. Pinelands and wet upland woods. Fla.—La., north to S. C.

Spurge Family   Euphorbiaceae

WILD POINSETTIA, PAINTED-LEAF   *Euphorbia heterophylla* L.

Closely related to the cultivated poinsettia, the wild poinsettia is a branched annual, 1—4 feet tall, with the leaves varying from narrow to ovate and from deeply lobed to smooth along the margins. The leaves that are borne immediately beneath the flower clusters are blotched with red or white at their base. The separate male and female flowers are clustered together in a manner that resembles a single flower. Several male flowers surround a single female flower, with no true perianth parts on either. Both the stems and the leaves contain a milky latex that flows freely when the plant is cut or bruised. June—November. Damp sandy soil, wooded slopes, and waste places. Fla.—Tex., north to Va. and Minn.

FLOWERING SPURGE   *Euphorbia corollata* L.

This spurge is a common, widespread perennial, 1—3 feet tall. As in most members of the spurge family, both the stems and the leaves exude a milky latex when bruised. What appears to be a single flower is a cluster of male flowers surrounding a single female flower. The structures that look like white petals are actually appendages of glands that surround the flowers. The central female flower, resembling a single pistil, continues to grow and eventually hangs outside the ring of male flowers. May—October. Open woods, fields, roadsides. Fla.—Tex., north to Can.

Yellow Milkwort

Low Bachelor's-Button

Wild Poinsettia

Flowering Spurge

ANDRACHNE   *Andrachne phyllanthoides* (Nutt.) Muell.

This shrub was unknown east of the Mississippi River until Blanche Dean recently discovered it growing along a stream in Blount County, Alabama. The branched stem grows to a height of 4 feet and has roots that run under rocks and boulders to the water's edge and into the stream. About an inch across, the thick alternate leaves are elliptic or rounded. The male and female flowers are borne on the same plant, the male flowers having larger petals, thus being more conspicuous. The fruit is a capsule that splits into three segments bearing six seeds. May—October. A very rare plant found on dry rocky hillsides and along stream banks. Blount County, Ala., and from southern Mo. to Tex.

QUEEN'S-DELIGHT, QUEEN'S-ROOT   *Stillingia sylvatica* Garden

This deep-rooted herb, 1—4 feet tall, bears several stems from a single crown. The toothed leaves are almost sessile and are elliptic to narrowly obovate. The male and female flowers are crowded into a terminal spike with the female flowers at the base of the spike and the male flowers above. The flowers have a 2—3 parted calyx, but no petals; the male flowers have 2—3 anthers, the female flowers, a single 3-lobed pistil. May—July. Dry woods, pinelands, and sand dunes on the Coastal Plain. Fla.—Tex., north to Va.

ALABAMA CROTON   *Croton alabamensis* E. A. Smith

Alabama croton is one of the rarest shrubs in the United States. Known from two river valleys in central Alabama, the Black Warrior and the Cahaba, within these valleys it is known only from Bibb and Tuscaloosa counties. It is sometimes locally abundant, however, forming dense thickets. The plants are semievergreen shrubs, 5—9 feet tall, with stems and leaves covered with silvery scales. The upper surfaces of the leaves are green, dotted with the silvery scales, whereas the undersides of the leaves are silvery white, due to the dense overlapping scales. The flowers are small and unisexual with both male and female flowers borne together in a terminal raceme consisting of 10—20 male flowers and 4—7 female flowers. The fruit is a silver, 3-lobed capsule about ⅓ of an inch in diameter. Peculiarly adapted to the rather harsh habitats of shale and limestone river bluffs with shallow soil and intense summer drought, Alabama croton completes most of its life cycle in early spring and essentially becomes dormant by early summer. Turning a beautiful orange in autumn, many of the leaves persist through the winter. February—March.

Queen's-Delight

Andrachne

Alabama Croton

Alabama Croton

TREAD-SOFTLY, SPURGE-NETTLE   *Cnidoscolus stimulosus* (Michx.) Engelm. & Gray

This nettle is an herbaceous perennial with sharp, stinging hairs covering the entire plant. The plants are usually 1−2 feet tall with palmately lobed, alternate leaves. The flowers are unisexual with both male and female flowers occurring on the same plant in a terminal cluster. The male flowers have a white perianth about an inch across that consists of sepals only. The sepals of the female flowers are shed very early, leaving only the 3-lobed ovary. March−September. Dry sandy woods, fields, and open areas. Fla.−Tex., north to Va.

Box Family   Buxaceae

ALLEGHENY SPURGE   *Pachysandra procumbens* Michx.

Growing from matted creeping stolons, this perennial herb is 6−18 inches tall and has scalelike lower leaves and coarsely toothed, ovate upper leaves, mottled with lighter green. Separate male and female flowers are borne on the same naked spike, with the female flowers at the base of the spike and the male flowers above. No perianth parts are formed on any of the flowers, but the male flowers are conspicuous with protruding anthers on long white filaments. March−April. Rich woods. Ala.−La., north to Ky.

Cashew Family   Anacardiaceae

POISON IVY   *Rhus radicans* L.

Anyone interested in studying wildflowers should learn to recognize quickly this and the following species. Poison ivy is a climbing vine with leaves divided into 3 elliptic or ovate leaflets that are usually shiny and are often shallowly lobed near the apex. Borne in the axils of the lower leaves are clusters of greenish flowers about ⅛ inch across that mature into small, white, berrylike fruits. April−May. Woods, roadsides, and waste places, throughout eastern North America. Poison oak, *Rhus toxicodendron*, has erect stems, and leaves that are thicker and usually more lobed. These two species and the following contain a volatile oil that causes dermatitis in susceptible persons.

POISON SUMAC   *Rhus vernix* L.

A large shrub or small tree up to 20 feet tall, poison sumac has smooth, powdery bark and pinnately compound leaves with 7−13 leaflets. The leaf stalks are often reddish, and there is an odd number of leaflets. Clusters of small, whitish fruits are borne in the axils of upper stem leaves. Though turning a beautiful orange or dark red in the fall, the leaves should be carefully avoided. May−June. Low, moist woods and swamps. Fla.−Tex., north to Can.

Tread-Softly

Allegheny Spurge

Poison Ivy

Poison Sumac

Titi Family   Cyrillaceae

BUCKWHEAT TREE, BLACK TITI   *Cliftonia monophylla* (Lam.) Britt. ex Sarg.

Cliftonia is an evergreen shrub or small tree, up to 25 feet tall, with scaly bark on the older trunks. The leaves are smooth, elliptic, and usually whitish beneath. Borne both terminally and in the axils of leaves are racemes of white flowers. Each flower is about ⅛ inch across with 5 petals and 10 stamens. The filaments of the stamens are distinctive, being broad and petallike below the middle. The fruits are 3—4 winged, somewhat resembling buckwheat. April—May. Acid bogs and swamps on the outer Coastal Plain. Ga.—Miss.

TITI, LEATHERWOOD   *Cyrilla racemiflora* L.

Titi is a semievergreen shrub or small tree with gray or reddish spongy bark. The thick, leathery leaves have a dense, netlike venation pattern on the upper surface. Numerous racemes, 4—12 inches long, are borne on second year growth. The flowers are about 1/16 inch across and have 5 white petals that bear glandular tissue on the inner surface and secrete a nectar that is attractive to bees. Small, berrylike drupes are greenish-yellow, turning brown and persisting until late fall. May—July. Sandy, acid soil on the Coastal Plain. Tex.—Fla., north to southern Va.

Buckeye Family   Hippocastanaceae

BOTTLEBRUSH BUCKEYE   *Aesculus parviflora* Walt.

This beautiful but rare species is easily distinguished from all other buckeyes by its elongate clusters of white flowers. Growing up to 15 feet tall, this shrub has leaves palmately divided into 5—7 leaflets. The white corolla is about an inch long, and the anthers have long filaments that extend over an inch beyond the corolla; thus the flower cluster has the appearance of a bottlebrush. May. Rich woods along stream banks. Ala.—Fla., north to S. C. The common red buckeye, *Aesculus pavia*, is easily distinguished by the red corolla that is strongly bilaterally symmetrical.

Soapberry Family   Sapindaceae

BALLOON-VINE, HEART-SEED   *Cardiospermum halicacabum* L.

The balloon-vine is an herbaceous or woody climber with alternate, coarsely toothed leaves that are twice divided into groups of 3 leaflets. The four petals have clawlike appendages near their bases. The green to golden bladderlike capsules are spherical to obovoid and reach a diameter of 3/16 inch. The seeds enclosed in the capsule bear a heart-shaped scar. July—September. Native to tropical America, this species has escaped from cultivation and become thoroughly naturalized in moist thickets and waste places, Fla.—Tex., north to N.J.

Buckwheat Tree

Titi

Bottlebrush Buckeye

Balloon-Vine

Touch-Me-Not Family   Balsaminaceae

JEWEL-WEED, TOUCH-ME-NOT   *Impatiens capensis* Meerb.

A freely branching annual herb up to 6 feet tall, jewel-weed has smooth, succulent, hollow stems. The flowers are irregular, consisting of a cornucopia-shaped perianth that is up to 1½ inch long and tapers to a curved spur. As is commonly true of species with red flowers and a long perianth tube, jewel-weed is often pollinated by hummingbirds. Both the common name and the Latin name refer to the manner in which the seed capsules burst open when touched. May—October. Wet woods and stream banks. Ga.—Okla., north to Can. *Impatiens pallida* has light yellow or cream colored flowers; *I. balsamea* has pubescent stems and pink or white flowers.

Buckthorn Family   Rhamnaceae

NEW JERSEY TEA   *Ceanothus americanus* L.

New Jersey tea is a low, bushy shrub up to 3 feet high with a reddish root. The alternate, ovate leaves are conspicuously veined and downy beneath. The small white flowers occur in dense, oblong, umbellike clusters on terminal or long, axillary stalks. The hooded petals are clawed at base and grow from a fleshy disc. The fruit is a 3-lobed drupe that is dark brown or nearly black at maturity. The leaves of this plant were used as a substitute for tea during the Revolutionary War. May—June. Dry open woods and rocky banks. Fla.—Ala., north to Can.

Mallow Family   Malvaceae

POPPY MALLOW   *Callirhoë triangulata* (Leavenw.) Gray

The poppy mallow is a perennial herb up to 2½ feet tall, covered with stellate hairs. It differs from all other species of *Callirhoë* in having undivided leaf blades with triangular or hastate bases. The 5 petals are purple or magenta and poppylike in general appearance, but as in the structure of a mallow, a column of stamens surrounds the ovary and style, and a five-parted stigma protrudes from the apex of the column. May—August. Dry woods and prairies. Ala.—Tex., north to N. C. and Wis.

CHEESES   *Modiola caroliniana* (L.) G. Don

The spreading, prostrate stems of this perennial are covered with stellate hairs and reach a length of up to 2 feet. The leaves are palmately 3—5 lobed and coarsely toothed. Opening only in sunlight, the flowers have 5 orange-red petals with a dark purple base. The flowers are solitary on axillary pedicels about an inch long, which elongate to 3 inches in fruit. There is only one species of this genus in eastern North America. March—June. Low ground, pastures, roadsides, Coastal Plain. Fla.—Tex., north to Va.

Jewel-Weed

New Jersey Tea

Poppy Mallow

Cheeses

Rose Mallow, Swamp Rose
Hibiscus moscheutos L.

The rose mallow is a tall perennial growing to a height of 6 feet. The leaves are serrate along the margins, and the lower leaves are sometimes 3-lobed. Occasionally finely pubescent and grayish above, the leaves are always densely hairy and grayish to almost white below. Axillary from the upper leaves, the large showy flowers have white or cream-colored corollas with red or purple centers. There is also a pink-petaled form with red centers. The fruit is a 5-chambered capsule. June—September. Marshes. Fla.—Ala., north to Md. and Ohio.

Swamp Mallow
Hibiscus aculeatus Walt.

This perennial is covered with short, stiff, white hairs and grows to a height of 6 feet. The leaves are deeply, palmately lobed into 3—5 coarsely and irregularly toothed segments. Changing in color progressively from cream to yellow and finally fading to pink, the 5 petals are marked with a purple or crimson spot at the base. The flowers are about 6 inches across and are borne in leafy racemes. The capsules are less than an inch long and are shaped like small okra pods. June—August. Pinelands, Coastal Plain. Fla.—La., north to N. C.

Wild Cotton, Swamp Mallow
Hibiscus palustris L.

This wild hibiscus grows to a height of 3—8 feet. Broadly ovate and usually 3-lobed, the leaves are green and smooth above and densely white-hairy beneath. The flowers have a musty odor and are borne in the upper leaf axils, with the flowering stalks fused to the leaf stalks for a short distance. The corolla is pink, purple, or rarely, white, with a dark red center. Each petal may reach a length of over 2 inches and the flower may be over 6 inches across. June—October. Salt or fresh-water marshes and wet banks. Ga.—Ala., north to Can.

Tea Family, Camellia Family
Theaceae

Silky Camellia
Stewartia malacodendron L.

Beautiful and rare, the silky camellia is a native shrub or small tree closely related to the Japanese *Camellia*. Typically it is 3—15 feet tall with simple, broadly elliptic to ovate leaves that are alternate, obscurely toothed, hairy beneath, and usually 1½—3 inches long. Axillary on short peduncles, the showy flowers measure 2—3 inches across and have 5 white petals with wavy margins. The stamens are numerous and fused basally by their purple filaments. The capsule is globular and bears lustrous seeds. May—June. Moist woods, stream banks. Western Fla.—La., north to Va. and Ark.

Swamp Mallow

Rose Mallow

Wild Cotton

Silky Camellia

MOUNTAIN CAMELLIA   *Stewartia ovata* (Cav.) Weath.

This camellia is another Southern shrub, similar to *Stewartia malacodendron*, but easily distinguished by a number of characteristics. The leaves are larger, 2—6 inches long, and ovate to widely elliptic with an acuminate apex. About 3½ inches in diameter, the solitary flowers are borne on short peduncles. Often having 6 petals, the flower has numerous stamens with yellow or purplish filaments and a pistil that is distinctive in having 4 styles. The seeds have an angular or crested margin. June—July. Rich woods and stream banks, mountains and Piedmont.Ga.—Ala., north to Va. and Ky.

St. John's-Wort Family   Hypericaceae

ORANGE-GRASS, PINEWEED   *Hypericum gentianoides* (L.) BSP.

A wiry annual herb that scarcely looks like a flowering plant, orange-grass gives off an odor of orange peel or pine needles when crushed, thus it has the common names orange-grass and pineweed. Growing to about a foot in height, it branches into many erect threadlike stems and has scalelike leaves that are only about 1/10 of an inch long. The small yellow flowers are up to ¼ inch across and are sessile along the sides and at the ends of branches. June—September. Sandy, rocky soil, fields, pastures, roadsides. Fla—Tex., north to Can.

ST. PETER'S-WORT   *Hypericum stans* (Michx.) P. Adams & Robson

This plant is a small erect shrub, 1—3 feet tall, with a simple or sparingly branched stem. About an inch long, the opposite leaves are elliptic or obovate with a broadly wedge-shaped or clasping base. The solitary flowers are axillary or in small clusters. There are four sepals, the outer two larger and enclosing the inner two. The stamens are numerous and borne in small groups. Less than ½ inch long, the ovoid capsules bear small brown seeds. June—October. Dry woods, pinelands, and ditches. Fla.—Miss., north to N. J. and Ky.

SPOTTED ST. JOHN'S-WORT   *Hypericum galioides* Lam.

This evergreen *Hypericum* is a shrub up to 5 feet tall and has leaves, petals, and sepals conspicuously marked with black dots. The leaves are opposite, linear to spatulate, often partly clasping at the base. The small flowers are crowded into dense, compact inflorescences. Very similar to *H. densiflorum*, this species differs primarily in having smaller leaves, fruits, and seeds. June—August. Swamps, stream banks, and low pinelands. Coastal Plain. Fla.—Miss., north to S. C.

Mountain Camellia

Orange-Grass

St. Peter's-Wort

Spotted St. John's-Wort

107

ST. ANDREW'S CROSS   *Hypericum hypericoides* (L.) Crantz

Only 1–3 feet tall, this small shrub has ascending branches and scaly older bark. The opposite leaves are elliptic to oblanceolate, up to an inch long. In the flower there are 4 sepals, two of which are very small or occasionally lacking, the other two being large and surrounding the capsule. The four petals are arranged in the shape of a cross, thus leading to the common name St. Andrew's cross. This is the cross represented on the Alabama state flag. The small ovoid capsules bear black seeds. May–August. Dry sandy soil. Fla.–Tex., north to Mass.

MYRTLE-LEAVED ST. JOHN'S-WORT   *Hypericum myrtifolium* Lam.

The myrtle-leaved St. John's-wort is very easily distinguished as it is the only shrubby *Hypericum* in Alabama with leaves that are strongly clasping at the base. An evergreen shrub up to 3½ feet tall, it has bright yellow flowers about an inch across. The sepals are leaflike with the 2 outer sepals larger than the 3 inner ones. The capsules are conical and about 1/16 inch long. June–July. Outer Coastal Plain in low pinelands and along pond margins. Fla.–Miss., north to S. C.

Rockrose Family   Cistaceae

FROSTWEED, ROCKROSE   *Helianthemum carolinianum* (Walt.) Michx.

An erect plant up to 10 inches tall, frostweed has a rosette of leaves at the base of the hairy stem and alternate, usually elliptic, leaves on the stem. About 2 inches across, having 5 yellow petals and 25–30 stamens, the flowers are few in a leafy raceme and remain open only for a single day and even then only in bright sunshine. March–June. Dry pinelands, Coastal Plain. Tex.–Fla., north to N.C. *Helianthemum corymbosum* has leaves that are silvery beneath and flowers in flat-topped clusters.

Violet Family   Violaceae

GREEN VIOLET   *Hybanthus concolor* (Forst.) Spreng.

The green violet is a perennial herb 1–3 feet tall with no resemblance to the typical violet. The stems are solitary or in small clusters, rising from fibrous roots. The leaves are alternate, elliptic, and usually 3–7 inches long. The small green flowers are in racemes of 1–3 on drooping stems in the axils of the middle leaves. The flowers are bilaterally symmetrical with 5 sepals, 5 petals, and 5 stamens. The sepals and lateral petals are similar in size and shape, but the lower petal is slightly longer and swollen at the base. Later in the season very small, cleistogamous flowers are borne in the axils of the upper leaves. As the name implies, these flowers never open and are thereby self-pollinated. April–June. Rich woods, calcareous slopes and ravines. Ga.–Miss., north to Can.

St. Andrew's Cross

Frostweed

Myrtle-leaved St. John's-Wort

Green Violet

Bird-Foot Violet
Viola pedata L.

The bird-foot violet is one of the stemless violets. That is, the stem, a short cormlike rhizome, is all underground, and the above-ground portion of the plant consists of leaves and flowers only. The leaves are palmately 3-parted with the lateral segments also frequently 3—5 parted. The flowers are usually 1—1¾ inches across, with violet to purple, rarely white, petals. The upper 4 petals commonly curve backward and are beardless, whereas the spurred petal may bear very short hairs. The stamens have very conspicuous orange tips. March—May. Dry, rocky or sandy soil, open woods, sunny sites. Fla.—Tex., north to Me. and Minn. There is a very common form in the state that is bicolored, with two dark, velvety-purple upper petals.

Wood Violet
Viola palmata L.

The wood violet is a stemless form growing from an elongate, stocky, often freely-branching rhizome. The leaves are palmately lobed or cleft into 5—11 segments, with the middle lobe broader than the others. The flowers are up to an inch across, deep blue-violet with a white center. Smaller cleistogamous flowers are often formed by this species, but not by the bird-foot violet. The capsules are ovoid, mottled, and bear brown seeds. March—May. Woodlands, dry rich soil, especially calcareous slopes. Fla.—Miss., north to Mass., and Minn.

Sweet White Violet
Viola blanda Willd.

This violet is a stemless plant with a slender stoloniferous rhizome. The glossy green, ovate leaves are up to 3½ inches long and have acute tips, crenate margins, and reddish petioles. Mildly fragrant, the flowers are up to ⅞ of an inch across and have white petals, the upper and lateral ones reflexed and the lateral ones usually half-twisted. The cleistogamous flowers are smaller and borne on erect or divergent peduncles. The purple capsules contain reddish to grayish black seeds. April—June. Rich, moist woods, cool ravines, mountains. Ga.—Fla., north into Can.

Common Blue Violet
Viola papilionacea Pursh

This is one of the most common violets in the Southeast. From a stout rhizome are borne leaves that are broadly cordate-ovate with crenate margins and membranaceous, or rarely, green stipules. Typically the 5 petals are violet or blue with a white base. The lateral petals are bearded with tufts of slender white hairs, but the spurred petal is beardless. Cleistogamous flowers are borne on erect to divergent peduncles. The capsules are ellipsoid and green to purple, with olive-brown to black seeds. February—May and occasionally in autumn. Woods, fields, roadsides. Fla.—Tex., north to Me. and N. D. This is a highly variable species and some authors recognize some of the variants as separate species. A white-flowered form (var. *priceana*), known as the Confederate violet, is often distinguished.

Bird-Foot Violet

Wood Violet

Sweet White Violet

Common Blue Violet

LONG-SPURRED VIOLET   *Viola rostrata* Pursh

Erect or spreading from a more or less branched rhizome, the nearly smooth stems of the long-spurred violet are 2—5 inches tall, elongating to a height of up to 10 inches after flowering. The leaves are ovate with cordate bases and acuminate tips. The petals are bluish-violet, often darker at the base. The spurred and lateral petals are veined with a deeper purple. The most distinctive feature of the flower is the spur, ½ inch or more long, extending either straight backward or curving upward from the lower petal. This spur distinguishes this species from all other violets. April—May. Rich moist woods. Ga.—Ala., north to Vt. and Wis.

HALBERD-LEAVED VIOLET   *Viola hastata* Michx.

The slender, smooth stems of the halberd-leaved violet grow 4—12 inches tall from pale, brittle rhizomes. Only 2—4 leaves are formed each year and these are distinctive, having cordate or hastate bases that give them the general shape of an arrowhead. Usually the leaves are variegated with silver-gray blotches between the veins. The stipules are typically triangular-ovate. Borne on slender axillary stems, the flowers are yellow with violet on the backs of the petals. Late March—May. Rich deciduous woods. Fla.—Ala., north to Pa. and Ohio.

PANSY, JOHNNY-JUMP-UP   *Viola tricolor* L.

A native of Europe, this species from which the cultivated pansy was derived is also cultivated and often escapes from cultivation. It is similar to and often interbreeds with another European species, *Viola arvensis*, giving an extremely wide variety of color patterns. Generally, *V. tricolor* has two purple upper petals and the other petals variously colored; whereas *V. arvensis* has petals that are primarily yellow, marked with other colors. Also, in *V. tricolor* the petals are 2—3 times the length of the sepals, whereas in *V. arvensis* the sepals and petals are about equal in size. March—June. Uncommon and not persisting for many years, roadsides and lawns, throughout eastern U. S.

FIELD PANSY   *Viola rafinesquii* Greene

The slender, smooth stems of this violet may grow to a height of 8 inches and are often branched from the base. The basal leaves are rounded and the stem leaves are more elongate and have smooth margins. The stipules are striking, being deeply divided into comblike divisions. Varying in color from bluish to cream-colored, the flowers are borne on long stalks. This is the only annual violet in the state and is often locally abundant in open areas. March—May. Fields, roadsides, open woods. Ga.—Tex., north to N. Y. and Mich.

Long-spurred Violet

Halberd-leaved Violet

Pansy

Field Pansy

DOWNY YELLOW VIOLET   *Viola pubescens* Ait.

This long-stemmed violet, sometimes growing to a height of 15 inches, has 1 or 2 softly hairy stems rising from a rhizome. Although usually leafless at the base, the plant may have a single basal leaf. The 2–4 stem leaves are very broadly ovate or rounded, blunt tipped, and coarsely toothed. The expanding leaves are downy. The flowers, borne on long axillary stems, have clear yellow petals with brownish-purple veins. The two lateral petals are bearded. The capsules are ovoid and usually densely hairy. May–June. Rich deciduous woods. Ga.–Miss., north to Me. and Minn.

Passion Flower Family   Passifloraceae

PASSION FLOWER, MAYPOP   *Passiflora incarnata* L.

Passion flower is a perennial vine, trailing or climbing by tendrils that arise opposite the leaves. These vines may grow to lengths of 10–20 feet. The alternate leaves have pairs of nectariferous glands at the base of the blades. Usually solitary, the axillary flowers are 2–3 inches across and have 5 sepals and 5 petals that are white to lavender and bear a crownlike outgrowth called a corona. The corona is fringed, the segments being white or lavender, banded with purple. Elevated above the other flower parts are the stamens and ovary, with the 3 styles terminating in globular stigmas. The ellipsoid berry, yellow at maturity, is commonly called a maypop and is edible. Symbolic significance has been attributed to various parts of this flower, usually in reference to the passion of Christ. May–July. Fields, roadsides, and open woods. Fla.–Tex., north to Va. and Ill.

YELLOW PASSION FLOWER   *Passiflora lutea* L.

This vine climbs by tendrils to a height of 10 feet or more. Shallowly 3-lobed with round apexes, the leaves are without glands on the petioles. The flowers are about an inch across and have a greenish-yellow perianth with a fringed yellow corona. The fruit is a small, round, purple to black berry about ½ inch in diameter and is not edible. June–September. Woodland borders, thickets. Fla.–Ala., north to Pa. and Kan.

Cactus Family   Cactaceae

PRICKLY PEAR   *Opuntia compressa* (Salisb.) Macbr.

The prostrate or spreading fleshy stems of the prickly pear are highly specialized for the retention of water. The leaves are soon deciduous, although they are evident in the picture at right. The major photosynthetic structure of this plant is the stem rather than the leaf. Covered with a heavy waxy coating, the stems bear small tufts of sharp, barbed bristles called glochids and often have larger spines as well. The perianth is only partly differentiated, the greenish sepals grading into the longer yellow petals. The edible purple to reddish-brown fruit is up to 2 inches long. May–June. Sandy or rocky open habitats. Ga.–Miss., north to Mass. and Minn.

Downy Yellow Violet

Passion Flower

Yellow Passion Flower

Prickly Pear

Loosestrife Family Lythraceae

PURPLE LOOSESTRIFE *Lythrum lineare* L.

A smooth perennial herb 1—4 feet tall, purple loosestrife is much-branched and has creeping basal offshoots. The narrow, linear to lanceolate leaves are up to 1½ inches long, sessile, and mostly opposite. Solitary in the axils of the leaves, the flowers have 4—6 pale lilac, or rarely, white petals. The stamens and styles occur in at least two forms. In the long-styled form, the stamens are included within the corolla, and the style protrudes; in the short-styled form, the stamens protrude, and the style is included. The flowers of a given plant will all be the same but require pollen from a different plant with a different style length to produce a fertile seed. July—October. Brackish and saline marshes, outer Coastal Plain. Fla.—Tex., north to L. I.

Melastome Family **Melastomaceae**

MEADOW BEAUTY, HANDSOME HARRY *Rhexia virginica* L.

This meadow beauty is distinguishable from the others in Alabama by its hairy, square, winged stems that may be as tall as 3 feet. Opposite and sessile, the leaves have ciliate margins. The flowers are rose-purple and about an inch across. Surrounding the fruit is an urn-shaped structure that has a short neck and distinctive teeth at the apex. May—October. Sandy swamps, meadows and fields. This is the most widespread and the most common of the species of *Rhexia* in Alabama. Fla.—La., north into Can.

MEADOW BEAUTY, DEER GRASS *Rhexia alifanus* Walt.

The tallest of the meadow beauties occurring in Alabama, this herbaceous perennial reaches a height of almost 4 feet. The sessile leaves are opposite, lanceolate, and distinctly 3-veined. The stems are smooth and bear terminal cymes of flowers with 4 sepals, 4 petals, and 8 stamens. The large, sickle-shaped anthers are up to ⅛ inch long. At maturity the capsules are surrounded by an urn-shaped outgrowth from the corolla. May—September. Savannas, low pinelands, Coastal Plain. Fla.—La., north to N. C.

YELLOW MEADOW BEAUTY *Rhexia lutea* Walt.

The only yellow-flowered species of *Rhexia* in Alabama, *R. lutea* is a slender, branching perennial that grows to a height of about 2 feet. The stems are 4-angled and covered with glandular hairs. Elliptic or obovate, the leaves are 3-veined and covered with irregular patches of hairs. The 4 oblique, yellow petals are ½ inch long. April—July. Moist pinelands, savannas, Coastal Plain. Fla.—La., north to N. C.

Purple Loosestrife

Meadow Beauty

Meadow Beauty

Yellow Meadow Beauty

Evening Primrose Family   **Onagraceae**

MORNING HONEYSUCKLE   *Gaura biennis* L.

Morning honeysuckle is a coarsely branched biennial with straggling stems that reach a height of 5 feet. The leaves are narrowly elliptic and usually 2–4 inches long. The flowers are white, sometimes turning pink and borne in clusters of spikes. Growing from the top of the ovary, the calyx and corolla are tubular for almost half their length, then open into 4 lobes. The petal lobes are slightly asymmetrical and clawed. The stigma is 4-lobed and surrounded by a cuplike border. The common name, morning honeysuckle, is a misnomer as these plants are related to evening primroses, not honeysuckles. June–October. Stream banks, fields, and roadsides, particularly in prairies. Ga.–Miss., north into Can.

EVENING PRIMROSE   *Oenothera biennis* L.

The evening primroses are a large and very complex group of flowering plants. Because of their unusual breeding system, the oenotheras present the botanist with a pattern of diversity that is next to impossible to classify according to conventional systems. *Oenothera biennis* is one of the largest species in the group, reaching a height of up to 7 feet. The golden-yellow flowers, up to 3 inches across, open in the evening and remain open during the early morning. The capsule is distinctive, being slightly angled and tapering to the apex. June–October. Fields, roadsides, waste places. Fla.–Tex., north to Nfld. and Minn. A closely related species, *O. grandiflora*, occurring in extreme south Alabama, has flowers with petals 1½ inches long.

PRIMROSE, BUTTERCUP   *Oenothera speciosa* Nutt.

This is a very showy, though somewhat weedy perennial with erect or spreading stems 1–2 feet tall and elliptic, irregularly lobed leaves. The flowers are 2–3 inches across and have white or pink petals with yellow centers. The club-shaped capsules taper downward and are angled or winged. May–July. Dry soil, prairies, fields, and roadsides. In some areas this species forms a dense carpet along roadsides and surrounding fields. Fla.–Tex., north to Va. and Mo.

SEEDBOX   *Ludwigia alternifolia* L.

The lanceolate leaves of the seedbox are alternate and borne on erect, usually smooth stems that reach a height of 4 feet. Borne singly on short stems in the upper leaf axils, the small yellow flowers are about ¼ inch across. There are 4 sepals, 4 petals, and 4 stamens. The common name seedbox is derived from the almost square, box-shaped capsule that sheds its seeds through a small pore at the top. May–October. Swamps, marshes, and low, wet woods. Fla.–Tex., north to Mass. and Mich.

Morning Honeysuckle

Primrose

Evening Primrose

Seedbox

PRIMROSE WILLOW, WATER PRIMROSE   *Ludwigia peploides* var. *glabrescens* (Kuntze) Shinners

The primrose willow is an aquatic perennial, forming large floating masses in shallow water. The smooth, creeping or floating stems root in or near water. The leaves are alternate and up to 3 inches long. The yellow flowers, up to an inch across, are borne in the axils of stem leaves. There are 4 sepals, 5 petals, and generally 8 stamens. The capsules are cylindric. This plant was named originally for Bernard de Jussieu, the gardener of Marie Antoinette and one of the early botanists who worked on a natural system of classification. May—September. Ponds and margins of sluggish streams. Coastal Plain. Fla.—Tex., north to N. C. and Kan.

Ginseng Family   Araliaceae

GINSENG, SANG   *Panax quinquefolium* L.

Ginseng is an herbaceous perennial, growing from a tuberous, spindle-shaped root to a height of 1—2 feet, and bearing 3—4 leaves in a whorl at the top of a bare stem. Each leaf is palmately divided into 5, rarely 3—7, leaflets. The small greenish flowers may be either bisexual or unisexual, and are borne in a terminal, solitary umbel. The mature berries are bright red, and about ½ inch in diameter. May—June. Rich, cool woods and ravines. Northern Fla.—La., north into Can. This native plant is now rare in many parts of its range because of extensive collecting of the roots. These are not widely used in this country but are shipped to China where they are valued for medicinal purposes. A related plant known as wild sarsaparilla, *Aralia nudicaulis*, is easily identified by its single compound leaf with 3 groups of 3 leaflets, black berries, and aromatic rhizome.

Parsley Family   Apiaceae

WATER PENNYWORT, NAVELWORT   *Hydrocotyle umbellata* L.

This low, aquatic or marsh plant has floating or creeping stems with leaves that are rounded with scalloped margins, and about 1½ inches in diameter. The petioles may be as long as 6 inches. White or cream-colored, the numerous minute flowers are borne in simple, compact umbels. The peduncles are as long as or longer than the petioles. April—September. Fla.—Tex., north to Mass. and Minn. The lawn pennywort, *Hydrocotyle sibthorpioides*, has smaller leaves and flowers in small umbels of 3—10 flowers.

SWEET CICELY, ANISE-ROOT   *Osmorhiza longistylis* (Torr.) DC.

Another herbaceous perennial with aromatic roots, sweet cicely grows to a height of 3 feet or more. The leaves are divided into 3 leaflets, each of which is subdivided into 3—5 coarsely toothed leaflets. In compound umbels with 3—6 rays, the small white flowers are borne on short peduncles that become over ½ inch long in fruit. The distinctive styles are longer than the petals. About ¼ inch long, the fruits are tapered at both ends. April—May. Moist deciduous woods. Ga.—Okla. and Colo., north into Can.

Primrose Willow

Ginseng

Water Pennywort

Sweet Cicely

121

RATTLESNAKE MASTER, CORN SNAKEROOT   *Eryngium yuccifolium* Michx.

A coarse perennial with stiff, narrow, sword-shaped leaves, rattlesnake master has basal leaves up to 3 feet long with parallel veins and sharp, prickly spines along the margins. The solitary stem grows erect to a height of 4 feet and is often branched above. The small white or greenish flowers are in compact heads and are concealed by stiff bracts. Several such heads are arranged in a terminal cyme. June—August. Open woods, sandy roadsides. Fla.—Tex., north to Conn. and Minn. *Eryngium integrifolium* has net-veined leaves and blue flowers; *E. prostratum* is a small creeping species with the flowering head longer than broad.

PEPPER-AND-SALT, HARBINGER-OF-SPRING   *Erigenia bulbosa* (Michx.) Nutt.

This small perennial grows to a height of 2—9 inches from a tiny globular tuber. The one or two leaves are only partly unfolded at the time of flowering. The leaf blades are divided into three leaflets, each of which is further divided into narrow segments, giving a fernlike appearance. White with brown stamens, the tiny flowers suggest a mixture of pepper and salt. The compound umbels produce fruits that are broader than long, laterally flattened, and lined with 5 slender ribs. February—May. Deciduous woods. Ala.—Miss., north into Can.

GOLDEN ALEXANDER   *Zizia aurea* (L.) Koch

Golden Alexander is a smooth perennial, 1—3 feet tall, with both the basal leaves and the stem leaves twice compound into groups of three. The individual leaflets are lanceolate and finely serrate. The many small yellow flowers are in loose, compound umbels with 6—20 branches. The central flower in each umbel is sessile. The mature fruits are oblong and ribbed. April—May. Alluvial woods and swamps, chiefly mountains and Piedmont. Ga.—Tex., north into Can. Plants of the closely related genus *Thaspium* can be distinguished from *Zizia* by having the central flower in each umbel stalked.

QUEEN ANNE'S LACE, WILD CARROT   *Daucus carota* L.

Although native to the Old World, the white, lacy umbels of Queen Anne's lace are a familiar sight over most of the U. S. and Canada. A bristly-stemmed, freely branched biennial growing to a height of up to 6 feet from a stout taproot, this plant has leaves that are pinnately decompound. The dense, flat-topped umbel of white flowers forms a lacelike pattern, with the umbel often centered with a small purple flower. In drying, the flower cluster curls inward, forming a cuplike "bird's nest." The fruit is ovoid and bristled. May—September. Fields, roadsides, and waste places, throughout the U. S.

Rattlesnake Master

Pepper-and-Salt

Golden Alexander

Queen Anne's Lace

Heath Family

Ericaceae

SPOTTED WINTERGREEN, PIPSISSEWA

Chimaphila maculata(L.) Pursh

Common in dry, acid woodlands, this evergreen plant has short stems, 4—8 inches tall, growing from a trailing rhizome. The dark green, leathery leaves are opposite, sharply serrate, and 1—2 inches long. Contrary to the common name, the leaves are white-striped rather than spotted. The fragrant flowers, 1—5 in number, are borne on nodding peduncles at the summit of the stem. The petals are waxy-white, and the 10 stamens each have a distinctly two-horned anther. The globose capsules are held erect at maturity. May—June. Upland forests. Ga.—Ala., north to Can.

INDIAN PIPE, GHOSTFLOWER

Monotropa uniflora L.

A plant entirely lacking in chlorophyll, Indian pipe probably derives all its nourishment from decayed vegetable matter in the soil. Growing 4—8 inches tall, the stems are typically waxy-white, but may be pinkish, reddish, pale yellow, or some combination of these colors. All turn black upon drying. Solitary and nodding at the summit of the stem, the bell-shaped flower has bractlike petals similar in color to the stem. The capsules are black and held erect at maturity. June—October. Leaf litter, upland woods and low moist woods. Fla.—Cal., north into Can. and Alaska.

PINESAP

Monotropa hypopithys L.

Pinesap, like Indian pipe, is a saprophyte lacking in chlorophyll, but differs in having bell-shaped flowers borne in a bracteate raceme atop the stem. The young raceme is nodding but soon becomes erect. The plants are tawny, yellow, pinkish, red, or some combination of these colors. The different color forms have different blooming seasons, with the tawny and yellow forms blooming early, and those marked with red blooming later. All turn black upon drying. May—October. Moist woods. Fla.—La., north into Can.

MOUNTAIN LAUREL

Kalmia latifolia L.

Growing to a height of 10—15 feet, this beautiful evergreen shrub has dark green, leathery, elliptic leaves 2—4 inches long. The flowers have a saucer-shaped, 5-lobed corolla that is about ¾—1 inch across and is usually pale pink but varies from dark pink to white. There are 10 stamens with the anthers held in small pockets in the corolla. After the flower opens, the anthers often spring free of these pockets. The fruit is a small capsule covered with sticky hairs. April—June. Rocky slopes and stream banks, usually in acid soil, sometimes forming dense thickets. Fla.—La., north to N. Y. and Ohio.

Indian Pipe

Spotted Wintergreen

Pinesap

Mountain Laurel

TRAILING ARBUTUS, MAYFLOWER   *Epigaea repens* L.

One of the most celebrated of all spring flowers, trailing arbutus has become rare over a large part of its range and is now protected by law in many states. A prostrate, shrubby perennial with spreading branches trailing over the ground, often forming large patches, the plant has thick, leathery, evergreen leaves. Appearing after the flowering period, the new leaves are green at first but turn a rusty color over the winter. The sweet-scented, waxy flowers are crowded in short, terminal, axillary spikes. White to pinkish, the corolla is tubular with 5 flaring lobes. February—May. Sandy and rocky acid soil, usually in dry woodlands. Fla.—Miss., north into Can.

ALABAMA AZALEA   *Rhododendron alabamense* Rheder

Alabama azalea is a deciduous shrub, 5—10 feet tall and has elliptic or oblanceolate leaves. Borne in clusters of 3—10, the flowers usually open at the same time that the leaf buds are opening. About an inch long, the white corolla often has a yellow center on the largest lobe. The margins of the corolla lobes are smooth and not undulate. April—May. Rich woods. Ala.—Ga., and S. C. The wild honeysuckle, *Rhododendron canescens* is very similar, differing primarily in having pink flowers.

Diapensia Family   Diapensiaceae

GALAX, WANDFLOWER   *Galax aphylla* L.

Galax is a genus native to the eastern U. S. and has but a single species. It is a stemless perennial, growing from an underground rhizome, producing a basal cluster of leaves. The leaves are evergreen, thick, and shining, and generally rounded in shape. They often show tints of bronze with age. The small white flowers are borne in racemes on 10—20-inch, leafless stalks. The stamens are united into a crownlike tube. For many years, the leaves of galax have been collected and sold in the florist trade, leading to a real scarcity of the species in some areas. May—July. Rocky woodlands. Ga.—Ala., north to Va. and Ky.

Primrose Family   Primulaceae

SHOOTING STAR   *Dodecatheon meadia* L.

This perennial has a basal rosette of light green leaves, 4—12 inches long, typically tinged with red at the base. The unusual flowers are borne in nodding clusters of 3—15 in the axils of a whorl of bracts. The white, lilac, or pink flowers are marked with yellow and red at the base of the strongly reflexed corolla lobes. The 5 united stamens are thus exposed and appear to be the point of the "shooting star." The mature capsules are reddish-brown and erect. Late March—May. Rich moist woodlands and bluffs, usually on basic or neutral soils. Ga.—Tex., north to Pa. and Wis.

Trailing Arbutus

Galax

Alabama Azalea

Shooting Star

127

FRINGED LOOSESTRIFE   *Lysimachia ciliata* L.

Growing from a slender rhizome and reaching a height of 1−4 feet, this erect perennial
has opposite leaves that are 2−6 inches long and have long, ciliate-fringed petioles and
pointed tips. The bright yellow flowers are borne singly on long slender flower stalks
that arise in the axils of the upper stem leaves. The 5 corolla lobes are united at the base
into a tube. June−August. Swamps, marshes, damp thickets, stream banks. Fla.−N.
Mex., north into Can. Rare on the Coastal Plain.

WHORLED LOOSESTRIFE   *Lysimachia quadrifolia* L.

A single-stemmed perennial growing 1−3 feet tall, whorled loosestrife has sessile or
short-petioled leaves that are in whorls of 3−6. The whorled leaves, bearing flowers in
the axils, serve to distinguish this species from others closely related. Borne singly on
slender stalks, the small, star-shaped, yellow flowers have 5 petals with reddish spots
or streaks at their bases. The anthers have unequal filaments fused together at the base.
May−July. Open woods, shores, chiefly mountains and Piedmont. Ga.−Ala., north
into Can. Creeping Charlie, *Lysimachia nummularia*, has rounded leaves and a
trailing, prostrate stem, rooting at the nodes.

SCARLET PIMPERNEL, POOR MAN'S WEATHERGLASS   *Anagallis arvensis* L.

The scarlet pimpernel is a low, much-branched, winter annual with loosely spreading,
ascending or erect stems, 4−12 inches long. The leaves are opposite, sessile, and ovate,
¼−1¼ inches long. The flowers are borne singly on long flowering stalks that arise
from the axils of upper stem leaves. The wheel-shaped corolla has a small tube and 5
large lobes that are scarlet or rarely blue, with very small teeth along the margins. The
flowers of this plant close quickly with the darkness of an approaching storm but open
again when the sun reappears. A native of Eurasia, it has long been known in Europe as
poor man's weatherglass. April−November. Fields, roadsides, and disturbed sites.
Throughout the U. S. and Can.

Sweetleaf Family   **Symplocaceae**

SWEETLEAF, HORSE SUGAR   *Symplocos tinctoria* (L.) L'Her.

A deciduous or semievergreen shrub or small tree, sweetleaf is seldom found in areas
accessible to cattle because of their fondness for the sweet leaves. The leaves are oval,
up to 6 inches long, and often persist through the winter and into the spring flowering
season. Borne in dense clusters along the branches of the previous season's growth, the
small fragrant flowers have 5 yellow or orange petals and numerous stamens with
elongate filaments and orange anthers. The fruit is a cylindrical drupe, about an inch
long. March−April. Rich woods, particularly bottomlands. Fla.−Tex., north along the
coast to Del.

Fringed Loosestrife

Whorled Loosestrife

Scarlet Pimpernel

Sweetleaf

Styrax Family   Styracaceae

SILVERBELL   *Halesia carolina* L.

Silverbell is a shrub or small tree growing up to 25 feet tall and having elliptic leaves
that are finely toothed along the margins. The flowers, borne in clusters of 3—5, have
translucent-white, bell-shaped corollas about ¾ inch long. There are 8—16 stamens
fused basally into a single cluster. The fruit is 4-winged and about 1½ inches long.
March—May. Rich woods, stream banks. Fla.—Tex., north to Va. *Halesia parviflora*
has a corolla only about ½ inch long with the style strongly protruding.

Olive Family   Oleaceae

FRINGE TREE, GRANDSIR-GRAYBEARDS   *Chionanthus virginicus* L.

A deciduous shrub or small tree up to 25 feet tall, the fringe tree appears festooned with
lace when it is in full bloom. The leaves are opposite and usually elliptic, becoming
somewhat thick with age. Numerous open panicles of white flowers are formed all over
the plant in the axils of leaves of the previous growing season. Very fragrant when they
first open, the flowers have 4 linear, strap-shaped petals about an inch long and two
elongate stamens. April—May. Dry and moist woods, often in acid soil. Fla.—Tex.,
north to N.J., often spreading from cultivation elsewhere.

Logania Family   Loganiaceae

YELLOW JESSAMINE, EVENING TRUMPET-FLOWER   *Gelsemium sempervirens*
                                                                 (L.) Ait. f.

A woody, high-climbing vine, yellow jessamine is one of the most beautiful and well-
known vines of the South. Although generally climbing by twining upward, the vines
may form dense, tangled mats by trailing over shrubs, rocks, or even bare ground. The
evergreen leaves are opposite, 1—3 inches long, and pointed at the tips. The fragrant,
bright yellow flowers are axillary and either solitary or in short clusters. The petals are
united into a funnel-shaped tube with 5 spreading, rounded lobes. March—early May.
Wet or dry woodlands, thickets, and roadsides, Fla.—Tex., north to Va. and Ark. A
very similar species, *Gelsemium rankinii*, also occurs in the state and can be
distinguished by its odorless flowers with sharp-pointed sepals.

INDIAN PINK, PINKROOT   *Spigelia marilandica* L.

Indian pink is an erect, perennial herb up to 2½ feet tall with opposite leaves that are
sessile or nearly so. The flower cluster is a terminal, one-sided cyme of trumpet-shaped
flowers, each 1—1¾ inches long. Scarlet outside and greenish-yellow within, the
corolla tube is terminated by 5 sharp-pointed lobes. Both the stamens and the style
protrude from the corolla. This beautiful wildflower is easily transplanted into areas of
partial shade but should be protected because it contains a poisonous alkaloid.
May—June. Rich woodlands. Fla.—Tex., north to Md. and Ind.

Silverbell

Fringe Tree

Indian Pink

Yellow Jessamine

Gentian Family   Gentianaceae

Pennywort   *Obolaria virginica* L.

Pennywort is a small fleshy perennial herb with brownish-purple stems up to 6 inches tall. The leaves are opposite, the lower ones scalelike, the upper ones fleshy, purplish, oval to triangular, and about ½ inch long. The flowers are white to purple, borne in terminal and axillary clusters of 3—5 blooms. The corolla is about ½ inch long with the 4 petals united for about a third of their length. This plant is easily overlooked in early spring under leaf litter. March—April. Rich moist woods. Mountains and Piedmont, rare on the Coastal Plain. Fla.—Tex., north to N.J. and Ill.

Colombo   *Swertia caroliniensis* (Walt.) Kuntze

Colombo is a smooth perennial with hollow stems growing 3—9 feet tall from thick tuberous roots. The lanceolate leaves are whorled, with 3—9 leaves per whorl. The flowers are in large, leafy, terminal clusters up to 3 feet long. Both the calyx and the corolla are 4-lobed. The yellowish to cream-white corolla is streaked with green and marked with brownish-purple dots. Near the base of each corolla lobe is a conspicuous green gland surrounded by a ciliate margin. This species is rare and should be protected. It is presently included on the U.S. Department of Agriculture list of flowering plants that will probably become extinct within a few years. May—June. Woodlands, often in calcareous soil. Ga.—La., north into Can.

Rose Pink, Bitter-Bloom   *Sabatia angularis* (L.) Pursh

Growing to a height of almost 3 feet, this much-branched annual has a 4-angled, often winged stem. The stem leaves are opposite, sessile, and ½—2 inches long. The flower cluster is a panicle of bright pink, or rarely, white flowers that are about an inch across. There are 5 sepals, 5 petals, and 5 yellow anthers. At the base of the petals is a central yellow starlike "eye" bordered with a thin red line. The sepals are lance-shaped, extending beyond the ovary almost the length of the petals. July—August. Woodlands, marshes, and fields. Fla.—La. and Okla., north to N.Y. and Wis.

Large Marsh Pink   *Sabatia dodecandra* (L.) BSP.

This marsh pink is a slender perennial with round or slightly angular, alternate branches, up to 2½ feet tall. Basal leaves may be present or absent and the stem leaves are opposite and lanceolate, ¾—2inches long. Borne on long slender branches, the flowers are about 3 inches across and are pink, or rarely, white with a red-margined, yellow center. The number of sepals, petals, and stamens varies from 8—13, although the name *dodecandra* implies that there are 12 stamens. June—September. Saline, brackish, or rarely, fresh-water marshes and meadows, primarily on the Coastal Plain. Fla.—La., north to Conn.

Pennywort

Colombo

Rose Pink

Large Marsh Pink

133

Bog Marsh Pink
Sabatia campanulata (L.) Torr.

A perennial with erect or spreading stems, bog marsh pink grows 1—2½ feet tall from a short rhizome. Basal leaves are absent. The stem leaves are linear-elliptic, ½—1½ inches long. The flowers are borne in an open, spreading panicle. The corolla, up to 1¼ inches across, is rose pink, rarely white, with a yellow "eye". June—August. Savannas and bogs. Ga.—Ala., north to Va. and Ind., and along the Coastal Plain to Mass.

Soapwort Gentian, Bottle Gentian
Gentiana saponaria L.

Soapwort gentian is an herbaceous perennial that derives its name from a resemblance to the true soapwort, *Saponaria*. Standing 1—3 feet tall, the glabrous stems of *Gentiana saponaria* bear flowers in terminal clusters as well as in the upper leaf axils or on short lateral branches. Blue or purplish in color, the corollas are tubular with lobes up to an inch long. The flowers are closed at first and even at maturity do not appear to be completely open. Late September—November. Moist woods, swamps, and bogs. Ga.—Tex., north to N.Y. and Minn. A closely related species, *G. catesbaei*, has corolla tubes that are open wide at maturity and a finely pubescent stem.

Sampson's Snakeroot
Gentiana villosa L.

The specific name of this plant is a misnomer as the stems are smooth rather than hairy. A perennial with stems 6—20 inches tall, Sampson's snakeroot has leaves that are opposite and elliptic. Greenish to yellow-white, and usually tinted or striped with purple, the corolla is funnel-shaped with the lobes loosely ascending. The flowers are almost sessile and are borne either singly or in compact cymes of 3—7 flowers. Late August—November. Open woods and pinelands. Fla.—La., north to N. J. and southern Ind.

Beautiful Gentian
Gentiana decora Pollard

A perennial that grows 1—2 feet tall from a thick, fleshy root, this gentian has a hairy, unbranched stem. The leaves are elliptic to lanceolate, narrowing to a point at the apex and at the base. The flowers are usually 3—12 in a terminal cyme or in smaller cymes among the upper leaf axils. Tubular or narrowly funnel-shaped, the corolla is blue, violet, or rarely, almost white, striped with blue or violet. September—October. Woods, coves, and stream banks, primarily in the mountains. Ga.—Ala., north to Va. and W. Va.

Bog Marsh Pink

Soapwort Gentian

Sampson's Snakeroot

Beautiful Gentian

Dogbane Family   Apocynaceae

BLUE STAR   *Amsonia tabernaemontana* Walt.

Usually growing in clumps from a woody rootstock, blue star is a smooth perennial
1—3 feet tall. Clustered in a terminal panicle, the flowers are star-shaped with short,
hairy tubes that separate above into 5 slightly contorted or rotated lobes. The petals are
blue on the outside and pale blue or white within. The leaves are alternate, which is
unusual for this plant family. Paired fruits, 2—4 inches long are held erect on the ends
of the flowering shoots. April—May. Rich woods and along stream banks, chiefly in
the Piedmont. Ga.—La. and Okla., north to Va. and Kans. A closely related species,
Amsonia ciliata, differs in having a hairy stem and a smooth corolla tube.

Milkweed Family   Asclepiadaceae

BUTTERFLY WEED, PLEURISY-ROOT   *Asclepias tuberosa* L.

This is an unusual member of the milkweed family because it does not have a milky
sap. It is an erect perennial, 1—3 feet tall with alternate leaves, 1—4 inches long, and
highly variable in shape. Yellow to orange or nearly red, the flowers are borne in
terminal or axillary umbels, usually in large numbers. The flowers of milkweeds are
rather complicated. The corolla lobes are reflexed, covering the sepals. The anthers are
united and fused to the stigma, and from the back of the united filaments arises a
structure consisting of 5 hoodlike appendages known as the corona. Within the corona
is a second appendage known as the horn. In *Asclepias tuberosa* the horns are shorter
than the hoods. May—August. Widespread in various habitats. Ga.—Tex. and Ariz.,
north into Can.

WHORLED MILKWEED   *Asclepias verticillata* L.

The whorled milkweed has numerous linear leaves that have curled margins and are
arranged in whorls along the stem. Growing 1—3 feet tall, the stems bear flowers in
small, terminal and axillary umbels. The corolla is greenish-white, with white hoods
that are about half the length of the incurved, claw-shaped horns. The pods are slender
and erect, 2—8 inches long. June—September. Dry open woods, sandhills, and
roadsides. Fla.—Tex. and Mex., north to Can.

WHITE MILKWEED   *Asclepias variegata* L.

The solitary, unbranched stems of the white milkweed stand 1—3½ feet tall. There
are 4—6 pairs of opposite leaves, 4—6 inches long with irregularly twisted margins.
The flowers are numerous in terminal and occasionally axillary umbels. The corolla
and the corona are white with a purple center. The horns are shorter than the hoods.
The seed pods are slender, 1—4 inches long. May—June. Open upland woods, chiefly
in the mountains and Piedmont. Fla.—Tex., north to Conn., Ill. and Mo.

Blue Star

Butterfly Weed

Whorled Milkweed

White Milkweed

MILKWEED   *Asclepias humistrata* Walt.

The smooth, stout, unbranched stems of this milkweed generally occur in spreading-ascending clusters 1–2½ feet tall. The opposite, sessile leaves, usually in 5–8 pairs, are ovate with small, earlike lobes at the base. The veins of the leaves are conspicuous and colored pink to lavender. The corolla is pale rose to lavender, with white hoods. The horns are slightly longer than the hoods. Borne erect, the seed pods are 3–5 inches long. May–June. Sandy dry pine-oak woods, sandhills, and dunes, primarily Coastal Plain. Fla.–Miss., north to N. C.

MILKWEED   *Asclepias lanceolata* Walt.

This is another of the unbranched, smooth-stemmed species of milkweed. Standing 2–4 feet tall, the plant has 3–6 pairs of opposite, lanceolate leaves and 2–4 umbels borne terminally or in upper leaf axils. The corollas are red, the hoods are a bright orange-yellow to scarlet, and the horns are much shorter than the hoods. Borne erect on deflexed stalks, the smooth pods are 3–4 inches long. June–August. Brackish marshes, swamps, and savannas. Coastal Plain. Fla.–Tex., north to N. J.

MILKWEED   *Asclepias amplexicaulis* Smith

This species is characterized by 1–3 erect, unbranched, smooth stems growing 2–4 feet tall from a root crown. There are 4–6 pairs of opposite, clasping leaves that are ovate and have wavy margins. Solitary and terminal, the umbels bear greenish-purple to rose-purple corollas with hoods that are pink and shorter than the horns. The pods are erect, 3–5 inches long. May–July. Open woods, clearings, roadsides, and fields. Fla.–Tex., north to Mass. and Minn.

SPIDER MILKWEED, ANTELOPE-HORN   *Asclepiodora viridis* (Walt.) Gray

This plant resembles *Asclepias*, but differs in having corolla lobes spreading or ascending rather than reflexed. Borne in several clustered umbels on stems that stand 1–2 feet tall, the flowers are without horns and have greenish corollas and purplish coronas. The alternate leaves are elliptic to lanceolate. The pods are 2–4½ inches long with soft, spiny protrusions. May–June. Pinelands, open woods, and prairies. Fla.–N. M., north to Can. and Neb.

Milkweed

Milkweed

Milkweed

Spider Milkweed

Morning-Glory Family Convolvulaceae

MORNING-GLORY *Ipomoea purpurea* (L.) Roth

One of the most well-known wildflowers is the high-twining morning-glory with its blue, white, purple, or variegated flowers. Introduced from tropical America, it has become established throughout the Southeast. The plant is a hairy annual with heart-shaped leaves and flowers borne in clusters of 1—5 in the axils of stem leaves. The length of the peduncle, the stalk bearing the flower cluster, is an important distinguishing characteristic in the morning-glories. In this species the peduncle is shorter than the petiole of the subtending leaf. The corolla is 1½—2½ inches long and about as broad. The stamens are included but the stigma protrudes from the corolla tube. July—September. Fields, roadsides, and waste places. Naturalized throughout the Southeast and infrequently beyond.

CYPRESS VINE *Ipomoea quamoclit* L.

Cypress vine is a smooth, twining annual with leaves that are pinnately divided into numerous narrowly linear segments. The flowers are 1—3 on stalks as long as the petiole of the subtending leaf. The corolla is scarlet, 1—1¼ inches long, and both the stamens and stigma protrude. August—October. Introduced from tropical America and now escaping along roadsides and in waste places. Throughout the southeastern U. S., north to Va. and Mo.

MAN-OF-THE-EARTH, WILD POTATO VINE *Ipomoea pandurata* (L.) Meyer

This perennial has an enlarged, starchy root that is truly remarkable, as it may be several feet long and weigh 20 pounds. Smooth to slightly hairy, the trailing stems are often purplish. The leaves are heart or fiddle-shaped. Clusters of 1—5 flowers are borne on peduncles longer than the petioles. The corolla is funnel-shaped, 2—3 inches long, and white with a tube that is purple within. The stamens and stigma remain well within the tube. May—July. Dry, open roadsides, fields, and waste places. Fla.—Tex., north to Conn., Mich. and Mo.

RAILROAD VINE *Ipomoea pes-caprae* (L.) Sweet

Native to the West Indies, this vine is a fleshy, perennial creeper with rounded leaves that are heart-shaped at the base, notched at the apex, and folded along the midvein. The name *pes-caprae* means goat foot, suggested by the folded leaf. The flowers are purple, 1½—2 inches long. Summer. Coastal sand dunes. Ga.—Fla.—Tex.

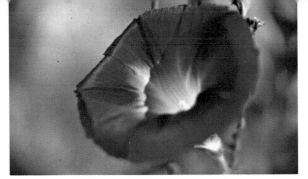

Morning-Glory

Cypress Vine

Man-of-the-Earth

Railroad Vine

ARROWLEAF MORNING-GLORY   *Ipomoea sagittata* Cav.

This glabrous, trailing or twining perennial has narrow, arrowhead-shaped leaves. Solitary, with rose-lavender, bell-shaped corollas, the flowers are 3—4 inches long. The stamens and stigma are include within the corolla tube. July—September. Moist sandy roadsides, swamps, and brackish marshes. Outer Coastal Plain. Fla.—Tex., north to N. C.

DUNE MORNING-GLORY   *Ipomoea stolonifera* (Cyrillo) Poir.

This perennial has smooth, trailing stems that often form roots at the nodes. Oblong or fiddle-shaped, the leathery leaves are slightly notched at the apex. The flowers are solitary on axillary peduncles that are about the same length as the petioles. The white, bell-shaped corolla is 1½—2 inches long, and about as broad. The stamens and style are included within the tube. August—October. Coastal sand dunes. Fla.—Tex., north to N. C.

HEDGE BINDWEED   *Calystegia sepium* (L.) R. Br.

This freely branched vine with arrowhead-shaped leaves and beautiful, white to rose-purple flowers is often mistaken for an *Ipomoea*. *Calystegia* is distinguished by having two separate stigmas that are thin and tapering and two large bracts that cover the calyx. The flowers are solitary with the corollas 1½—2¾ inches long and are borne in the axils of stem leaves. May—August. Fields, roadsides, and waste places. Fla.—N.M., north to Nfld. and Ore. *Calystegia spithamaea* has erect stems and few flowers, emerging from the axils of the lower leaves only. Another common weed similar to *Calystegia*, *Jacquemontia tamnifolia* has dense clusters of small blue flowers, each with 2 stigmas that are ovoid and not tapering.

Phlox Family   **Polemoniaceae**

SCARLET GILIA, STANDING CYPRESS   *Ipomopsis rubra* (L.) Wherry

Scarlet gilia is a biennial producing a large rosette of leaves the first year and a stout, erect stem up to 3 feet tall the second year. The leaves are alternate and pinnately divided into numerous linear or threadlike segments. The flowers, borne in slender, elongate clusters, have bright scarlet, or rarely, yellow corollas that are about an inch long and are tubular with 5 flaring lobes. The stamens are unequally protruding. This red flower with a long tube on a delicate stem is very well adapted for pollination by hummingbirds. June—August. Fields and margins of woods, usually in sandy soil. Coastal Plain and Piedmont. Fla.—Tex., north to N. C., often escaping from cultivation beyond this range.

Arrowleaf Morning-Glory

Dune Morning-Glory

Scarlet Gilia

Hedge Bindweed

WHERRY PHLOX   *Phlox pulchra* (Wherry) Wherry

The flowering stems of Wherry phlox are about a foot high, bearing broad, evergreen leaves, usually with six pairs on a stem. The flowers are soft pink and large, with a corolla tube about an inch long and the lobes each about ½ inch long. The stigmas are at least as long as the stamens, usually protruding from the tube. April—May. Roadsides and woods, very rare. Tuscaloosa, Walker, and Jefferson counties, Alabama.

DOWNY PHLOX   *Phlox pilosa* L.

The downy phlox is a slender perennial, 8—20 inches tall, with 2—5 branches from the upper nodes. There are 6—12 pairs of opposite, narrowly lanceolate leaves with ciliate margins. Borne in open clusters, the flowers have pink, lavender, or rarely, white corollas that are usually hairy within the tubes. The stamens are included, and the styles are cleft for approximately half their length. April—May. Dry woods, clearings and roadsides. Fla.—Tex., north to Conn., Mich., and Mo.

CAROLINA PHLOX   *Phlox carolina* L.

This species of phlox, with erect stems 1—3 feet tall, is quite variable. The leaves are opposite and vary from ovate to lanceolate, with smooth margins. The inflorescence is a large, rounded cluster of one-to-several cymes, with the lower flowers having long stalks. Lavender, pink, or rarely, white, the corollas are smooth within the tubes. The stamens protrude, and the styles are united. May—July. Very common in deciduous woods, savannas, and along roadsides. Fla.—Miss., north to Md. and Ill.

WILD SWEET-WILLIAM, BLUE PHLOX   *Phlox divaricata* L.

An early-blooming phlox of deciduous woods, sweet-William is a stoloniferous perennial with erect or sometimes bending, sterile and fertile stems. The fertile stems are 4—8 inches tall, twice as tall as the sterile stems. Characteristically there are 4 pairs of elliptic to lanceolate leaves on a flowering stem. The inflorescence is an open cluster of cymes. Both the calyx and the flower stalks are densely covered with glands. The pale lavender or bluish corollas are smooth within. The stamens are included, and the styles are cleft for approximately half their length. April—May. Rich deciduous woods. Ga.—Tex., north into Can.

Downy Phlox

Wherry Phlox

Carolina Phlox

Wild Sweet-William

145

JACOB'S LADDER, GREEK VALERIAN   *Polemonium reptans* L.

This is a tufted perennial 8–24 inches tall with erect stems and alternate, pinnately compound leaves with 11–21 elliptic segments. These ladderlike leaflets led to the common name Jacob's ladder. Pale lavender to white flowers are borne in loose, open clusters. The corolla is bell-shaped and the 3-lobed stigma protrudes. April–May. Moist deciduous woods and stream banks. Ga.–Miss. and Okla., north to N. Y. and Minn.

Waterleaf Family   Hydrophyllaceae

SCORPION-WEED   *Phacelia dubia* (L.) Trel.

Scorpion-weed is an erect or spreading annual 4–15 inches high with pinnately lobed or cleft leaves. Both the stems and leaves are covered with sharp, stiff hairs. The inflorescence is a coiled cyme with 10–30 pale blue to white flowers. The open, bell-shaped corolla has 5 lobes with smooth margins. March–June. Rich woods and thickets. Ala.–Ga., north to Del. and Pa. *Phacelia purshii* differs in having a pale blue or lavender corolla with a fringed margin. *Phacelia bipinnatifida* bears glandular hairs on the stem and leaves and has a corolla without the fringe.

HYDROLEA   *Hydrolea quadrivalvis* Walt.

Hydrolea is a perennial aquatic herb with fleshy, spiny stems. The leaves are elliptic and usually 2–5 inches long. Axillary cymes of blue flowers have bell-shaped corollas, each with 5 included stamens and 2 distinct styles. June–September. Marshes, river bottoms, and creek banks. Coastal Plain. Fla.–La., north to Va.

Borage Family   Boraginaceae

TURNSOLE, HELIOTROPE   *Heliotropium indicum* L.

The stem of this heliotrope grows 2–3 feet tall and bears an inflorescence 5–6 inches long with the small blue flowers all on one side. The inflorescence is a coiled spike that uncoils as the flowers open progressively from the base to the apex of the spike. The leaves are coarse and hairy, 2–4 inches long. The fruit is 2-lobed, each lobe containing one seed and one empty chamber. July–November. Native to Asia, this species has now become naturalized and widespread along roadsides, pastures, and ditches. Fla.–Tex., north to Va. A closely related species, *Heliotropium europaeum*, is similar but has a 4-lobed fruit with each lobe containing a single seed. The seaside heliotrope, *H. curassavicum*, is smooth and has linear leaves that are succulent; *H. tenellum* has stems and leaves covered with stiff white hairs and has small white flowers.

Scorpion-Weed

Jacob's Ladder

Hydrolea

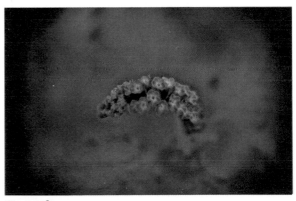

Turnsole

147

VIRGINIA BLUEBELLS, COWSLIP   *Mertensia virginica* (L.) Pers.

This native bluebell was named for the state where it was first discovered. It is a smooth perennial 1—2 feet tall with elliptic leaves that have long, tapering petioles at the base, becoming progressively shorter up the stem. Hanging in clusters from the curving tips of the branches, the funnel-shaped flowers are first pink and change to blue as they age, making a lovely combination of blue, pink, and green. March—June. Moist woods. Ga.—Ala. and Ark., north into Can.

VIPER'S-BUGLOSS, BLUE DEVIL   *Echium vulgare* L.

This is another attractive Old World species that has become widespread in this country and in some areas quite weedy. The bristly stems are 2—3 feet high, with linear, sessile leaves with bristles on both sides. The bright blue corolla, bristly as well, is irregular, with the upper lobe much longer than the lower. Extending beyond the corolla, the stamens have long red filaments that are striking against the blue corolla. Four of the filaments are noticeably longer than the fifth. Both the Latin name and the common name allude to the resemblance of both the corolla and the fruit to the head of a snake. June—October. Roadsides, fields, and wasteland, throughout the Southeast and north into Can.

HOARY PUCCOON   *Lithospermum canescens* (Michx.) Lehm.

The hoary puccoon has several stems that arise from a single thick taproot that is red or purplish. The stems are 1—1½ feet tall and, along with the leaves, are covered with soft hairs that lie flat against the surface. The flowers are bright yellow, about ½ inch across, and borne in terminal cymes. The fruits are smooth yellowish nutlets. April—May. Moist or dry open woods. Ga.—Tex., north into Can. A similar species, *Lithospermum caroliniense*, has larger flowers that are hairy within and has stiff bristly hairs on the stems and leaves.

Vervain Family   Verbenaceae

HOARY VERVAIN, VERBENA   *Verbena stricta* Vent.

Verbena stricta, an erect perennial with angled stems up to 3 feet tall, appears whitish due to the dense covering of white hairs on the stems and leaves. Usually sessile, the leaves are elliptic or ovate, thick, and coarsely toothed. The bright blue-violet flowers are ⅓ inch in diameter and borne on a slender spike 4—8 inches long with a rounded apex. June—September. Infrequent in open rocky places, fields, and prairies. Ga.—Tex., north to Can. and Mont.

Virginia Bluebells

Hoary Puccoon

Viper's-Bugloss

Hoary Vervain

STIFF VERBENA   *Verbena rigida* Spreng.

Stiff verbena is an erect plant with underground stolons that often form dense patches
several feet across. Wedge-shaped or clasping at the base, the elliptic leaves are 2—3
inches long, with a few sharp teeth along the margins. The upper and lower surfaces of
the leaves are rough to the touch. Borne in dense spikes about 2 inches long that are
held stiffly erect, the flowers are violet to purple, each with a tube about ½ inch long,
terminating in lobes that are about ¼ inch across. March—July. This is a native of
South America that has become widespread in waste places, particularly along
roadsides. Fla.—La., north to N.C.

ROSE VERVAIN   *Verbena canadensis* (L.) Britt.

The stem of the rose vervain is 1—2 feet long, lax, often bending to the ground and
rooting at the nodes. The leaves are variable in shape but are always opposite, deeply
lobed, and toothed. Large for verbenas, the flowers are each about ½ inch across,
varying in color from rose to violet. They are borne in dense, terminal spikes that are
flat-topped during the flowering period, elongating later. March—May. Roadsides,
sandhills. Ga.—Tex., north to Va. and Kan.

BRAZILIAN VERBENA   *Verbena brasiliensis* Vell.

This verbena is an erect perennial with a stout, smooth, 4-angled stem that may reach a
height of 6—8 feet. The smooth leaves are elliptic or lanceolate and taper gradually to
the base. The flowers are violet to purple, about ⅛ inch across, and borne in dense,
compound, terminal spikes, about an inch long. April—October. A native of South
America, now naturalized and widespread in dry, sandy soil, old fields, and disturbed
sites. Ga.—La., north to Va. A closely related species, *V. bonariensis*, is very similar but
can be distinguished by its rough stems, and by the leaves that are downy beneath and
have a sessile, clasping base.

FROG-FRUIT, CAPE WEED   *Lippia nodiflora* (L.) Michx.

Frog-fruit is a creeping herb with 4-angled stems up to 3 feet long, bearing short,
ascending, upright branches. The leaves are spatulate and toothed along the margin.
Small white or lavender flowers are borne in dense heads that are held erect above the
leaves. The flowers on the outside of the head bloom first, those toward the center later.
Late May—November. Damp sandy soil, Coastal Plain. Fla.—Tex., and Mex., north to
Va. and Mo. A similar species, *Lippia lanceolata*, can be distinguished by its leaves that
are lanceolate, tapering gradually toward the base and the apex.

Stiff Verbena

Rose Vervain

Brazilian Verbena

Frog-Fruit

Mint Family   Lamiaceae

HENBIT   *Lamium amplexicaule* L.

Henbit is one of the most common and widespread annual mints in the state. Although lacking the minty aroma, it does have the characteristic square stems, opposite leaves, and 2-lipped corollas. The plants are usually about 6–10 inches tall, with several stems arising from a single root. Rounded with crenate margins, the leaves are long-petioled at the base of the plant, becoming sessile on the upper stems. The flowers are about ½–¾ inch long with pink to purple lips, the upper lip being hairy. The first flowers produced never open but do form fertile seeds by self-pollination. February–May. A native of Europe that has now become widespread in fields, lawns, and waste places. Ga.–La., north to Can. *Lamium purpureum* can be distinguished by its upper leaves that are distinctly petioled.

BLUECURLS, BASTARD PENNYROYAL   *Trichostema dichotomum* L.

Bluecurls is an upright annual herb, 2–3 feet tall, that is sticky to touch because of the long-stalked, glandular hairs on the stems and leaves. The leaves are oblong to rhombic-lanceolate. The blue corolla is 2-lipped and has a 4-lobed upper lip and a broad, oblong lower lip. The curls of bluecurls are the long, curved, bluish filaments of the stamens. July–September. Dry fields, pinelands. Fla.–La., north to Conn. and Pa. *Trichostema setaceum* is similar but has linear leaves that are smooth or nearly so.

SKULLCAP, HELMETFLOWER   *Scutellaria integrifolia* L.

Skullcaps are easy to recognize by the hump or shield on the upper side of the calyx. They do not have the minty aroma characteristic of most members of the family. This species grows to a height of about 2 feet and has densely hairy stems with narrow, sessile, smooth-margined leaves. The upper lip of the flower is longer than the shallowly notched lower lip. The corolla is about an inch long, blue-violet with a white underside. May–July. Roadsides, pine barrens, open woods. Ga.–Miss., north to Mass. and Pa. *Scutellaria parvula* is a low-growing, stoloniferous species with leaves less than an inch long and axillary flowers less than ½ inch long. *Scutellaria alabamensis* has smooth leaves with toothed margins and a calyx with glandular hairs.

HEAL-ALL, SELF-HEAL   *Prunella vulgaris* L.

Heal-all is an attractive, but weedy, herbaceous perennial 1–2 feet tall. Although this species is highly variable, it is still easily distinguished by the dense, spikelike clusters of flowers. Varying in color from blue to violet to white, the flowers are separated by broad, toothed bracts. The corolla is almost an inch long, 2-lipped, with the upper lip forming a concave hood. April–October. Common throughout the U. S. and southern Can.

Henbit

Bluecurls

Skullcap

Heal-All

BEE BALM, OSWEGO TEA   *Monarda didyma* L.

This bee balm, the most brightly-colored of the monardas, has a corolla that varies
from scarlet to crimson. Growing to a height of 2 feet or more, it is a perennial with
square stems that are rough and hairy. The flowers are borne in dense, headlike cymes
that are usually solitary but occasionally bear a second cyme above the first. The
corolla is 2-lipped with the upper lip long and pointed and the lower lip broad and
recurved. The stamens are borne in pairs within the throat of the corolla. It was this
characteristic that Linnaeus alluded to with the name *didyma* meaning twin. July—September. Moist areas, particularly along seepage banks. Ga.—Ala., north to N.
Y.

WILD BERGAMOT, BEE BALM   *Monarda fistulosa* L.

Wild bergamot is similar to *Monarda didyma* and is much more common in Alabama.
It is a perennial herb, 1—5 feet tall, with leaves that are lanceolate and densely covered
with long silky hairs. The flowers are borne in a dense, headlike cluster that is usually
solitary. The corolla is lilac, purple, or rarely, white. The tip of the upper lip is bearded.
June—September. Roadsides, open woods, and meadows. Ga.—Tex., north into Can.

DOTTED HORSEMINT, DOTTED MONARDA   *Monarda punctata* L.

This monarda has a stem 1—3 feet high with lanceolate leaves that are downy and have
distinct petioles. The flower cluster consists of 2—7 headlike cymes, one above the
other with a short separation between each cyme. The bracts of the inflorescence are
lilac or whitish, and the flowers are pale yellow or cream-colored with bright purple
spots. July—October. Open sandy places, rocky woods. Ga.—La., north to N. Y.

LEMON MINT   *Monarda citriodora* Cerv. ex. Lag.

Lemon mint resembles *Monarda punctata* in having multiple vertical clusters of
flowers. An annual species, it has sharp-pointed bracts that are purple, lavender, or
white and form a cup around the flower. About ¾ inch long, the flowers are bluish to
lavender with darker purplish spots. June—August. Uncommon, found primarily on
calcareous soil. Ala.—Tex., north to S. C. and Kan.

Bee Balm

Wild Bergamot

Dotted Horsemint

Lemon Mint

155

WOOD MINT   *Blephilia ciliata* (L.) Benth.

Blephilia is a leafy-stemmed perennial somewhat resembling the monardas, but can be distinguished by its axillary as well as terminal flower clusters. It also differs in having a 2-lipped calyx with 3 spiny-tipped teeth on the lower side and 3 teeth on the upper side. The stem is 1−3 feet tall with downy leaves that are widest near the middle. Pink to purplish, the flowers have stamens that project beyond the corolla. *Blephilia* is from the Greek word for eyelash, referring to the fringe of long hairs on the edge of the bracts. Meadows and woodlands. May−July. Ga.−Tex., north to Vt. and Wis. *Blephilia hirsuta* has rounded leaves with long petioles and pale lavender flowers.

RED BASIL   *Satureja coccineum* (Nutt.) Kuntze

Red basil is a low shrub, up to 3 feet tall, with leaves about ¾ inch long, widest near the apex. The flowers are solitary with the bright scarlet corolla about 1½ inches long. The lobes of the upper lip of the corolla are shorter than those of the lower lip. Flowering throughout the year on dunes and sandy shores of the outer Coastal Plain, Ga., Fla., Ala. *Satureja georgiana* is also a shrubby species but has elliptic leaves and pink to lavender flowers. An herbaceous species, *S. glabella* is smooth except at the nodes, and has linear or elliptic leaves. In *S. vulgaris* the inflorescence is composed of 2−3 pairs of dense clusters of 8−10 rose to lavender flowers about ½ inch long.

MOUNTAIN MINT   *Pycnanthemum muticum* (Michx.) Pers.

There are a number of mountain mints in the state that are difficult to distinguish. This common species has ovate, toothed leaves on short petioles, is grayish-white on the stems and upper leaves, and has fine hairs on the stems. The calyx has very short teeth that are triangular. The corolla is white, speckled with purple. When bruised, the stems and leaves have a strong minty odor. June−August. Low meadows, bogs, woods. Ga.−Tex., north to Me. and Mich.

HORSE BALM, RICHWEED   *Collinsonia canadensis* L.

Horse balm is a coarse perennial herb, 5−15 inches high with thick tuberous roots. Distinctly 4-angled, the stems bear long-petioled leaves that are ovate to elliptic. The yellow flowers are about ½ inch long and have 2 long stamens protruding high above the corolla. The corolla is 2-lipped with the lower lip 3-lobed. The flowers and leaves have a pleasant lemonlike fragrance. June−August. Rich woods. Fla.−Ark., north to Mass. and Wis. A related species, *Collinsonia verticillata*, is easily distinguished by the 4 stamens of the flower.

Wood Mint

Red Basil

Mountain Mint

Horse Balm

Nightshade Family   Solanaceae

SILVERLEAF NIGHTSHADE   *Solanum elaeagnifolium* Cav.

This spiny herbaceous perennial has narrowly lanceolate leaves that are about 3 inches long and densely covered with starlike branched hairs, giving the plant a silvery sheen. The hairs are distinctive, having 12 or more rays. Freely branching, this plant grows to a height of about 2 feet. The flowers have lavender to purple corollas about an inch across, often with the lobes reflexed. June—September. A Southwestern species that has recently spread into the South. Fla.—Tex., north to Ohio and Kan. *Solanum carolinianum* also has spiny stems and leaves but is easily distinguished by its ovate leaves and by its hairs with 4—8 rays. The Irish Potato, *S. tuberosum*, occasionally escapes from cultivation, but does not persist.

GROUND CHERRY   *Physalis heterophylla* Nees

The ground cherry is a densely hairy plant with sticky glandular hairs intermixed with both long and short, non-glandular hairs. It is widely branched and has ovate leaves that are lobed, toothed, and rather thick. The yellow corolla is ½—¾ inches across and has 5 dark brown spots near the base. The calyx becomes enlarged and bladderlike in fruit, enclosing the berry. The name *Physalis* is from the Greek for bladder. The small edible berry or "ground cherry" is used in making pies and preserves. May—July. Woodlands, roadsides, and clearings. Ga.—Tex., north into Can. *Physalis angustifolia* has small linear leaves and a yellow corolla without the blotches inside.

MATRIMONY VINE   *Lycium carolinianum* Walt.

This plant is a vinelike shrub with a woody base and recurving branches. About ¼ inch wide, the leaves are succulent, entire, and grow in clusters on small side shoots. The flowers are usually solitary with blue or lavender corollas and protruding anthers and stigmas. The berries are ellipsoid and bright red. September—October. Sandy beaches and shell mounds. Fla., Ala., and S. C.

Snapdragon Family   Scrophulariaceae

COMMON MULLEIN, FLANNEL PLANT   *Verbascum thapsus* L.

This mullein is a common biennial of dry fields and roadsides. From a basal rosette of leaves arises a stem 6 feet or more tall with leaves that become progressively smaller up the stem. The stem terminates in a long spike of yellow flowers. The entire plant is covered with soft, white, woolly hairs that are branched one or more times. The pale yellow flowers are slightly irregular, with the lower petals longer than the upper ones. June—September. A native of the Old World that has now become naturalized throughout the U. S. and much of Can.

Silverleaf Nightshade

Ground Cherry

Matrimony Vine

Common Mullein

Moth Mullein
Verbascum blattaria L.

The moth mullein has slender stems about 3–4 feet tall. The stem is sometimes branched and is covered on the upper part with hairs that are glandular and sticky but not branched. The stem leaves are smooth, toothed, and 3–5 inches long. The flowers are yellow or white and simulate a moth—the lower two hairy stamens and the style resembling the antennae and tongue. April–June. This is another European native that has become naturalized over much of the U. S.

Turtlehead, Snakehead
Chelone glabra L.

A perennial with upright branching stems, turtlehead is well named since its flower strongly resembles the head of a reptile. Growing to a height of 4–6 feet, it has sessile leaves that are toothed and long-pointed. The flowers are white or ivory, tinged with purple, pink, or yellow, and are borne on a spike 2–3 inches long. August–October. Stream banks, low fields, and woodlands. Ga.–Miss., north into Can. *Chelone obliqua* also occurs in the same area and is readily distinguished by its smaller size, short-stalked leaves, and red-purple or purple corolla.

Seymeria
Seymeria cassioides (Geml.) Blake

A branching annual that often has a bushy appearance, *Seymeria* grows to a height of 2–3 feet and bears leaves that are pinnately divided into long threadlike leaflets. The flowers are about ½ inch across with pale yellow corollas divided into 5 almost equal lobes. This plant is thought to be a partial parasite. August–October. Sandy pinelands. Fla.–La., north to Va. and Tenn. *Seymeria macrophylla* has large leaves that are pinnately divided into lanceolate segments and a corolla tube that is woolly inside. *Seymeria pectinata* has a corolla that is smooth on the exterior and has winged seeds.

Hairy Penstemon
Penstemon hirsutus (L.) Willd.

Penstemon is an erect perennial herb with a basal rosette of petioled leaves, and stem leaves that are opposite and sessile. The tubular corolla is 2-lipped, the upper lip 2-lobed, the lower 3-lobed. There are 5 stamens, one of which is sterile and highly modified, usually bearing a tuft of hairs. In *P. hirsutus* the stem grows 1–3 feet high, is covered with whitish, gland-tipped hairs, and bears lanceolate, clasping leaves. The corolla is purple to pale violet with white lobes. Two ridges on the lower lip, known as a palate, arch upward, almost closing the corolla tube. May–July. Dry rocky soil. Ala.–Miss., north inland to Wis. and Ont.

Moth Mullein

Turtlehead

Seymeria

Hairy Penstemon

BEARD-TONGUE
Penstemon calycosus Small

Beard-tongue is usually about 3 feet tall with a somewhat purplish stem covered with soft downy hairs. The leaves are thin and sharply toothed. Long, tapering sepals about ½ inch in length spread outward at the tip. Over an inch long, the corolla is violet outside and almost white within. The anthers are smooth. May—July. Woods, meadows, limestone outcrops. Ala., north to Ill. and Ohio.

PENSTEMON
Penstemon digitalis Nutt.

This is a handsome species, 2—5 feet tall, with purplish, shining stems. The leaves have thin lines of hairs on the underside; those borne on the stem are thick and somewhat leathery. Leafy clusters of flowers arise near the apex of the stem with as many as 50 flowers on a stem. The corolla is lavender on the outside, and white within, often with a few darker purple lines within. The throat of the corolla is strongly inflated. The four fertile stamens have anthers that are distinctly hairy on the ends. May—June. Open woods, meadows, and prairies. Ala.—Tex., north to Me. and S. D.

SMALL'S PENSTEMON
Penstemon smallii Heller

Similar to *Penstemon digitalis*, this plant is more hairy and the hairs are glandular. The stem leaves are evenly toothed, with heart-shaped, clasping bases. The corolla is purple, becoming lighter toward the tube, with purple lines inside. The sterile stamen is bearded for about half its length with long yellow hairs. May—June. Wooded slopes and shaded bluffs. Ga.—Ala., north to S.C. and Tenn.

SMOOTH FOXGLOVE
Aureolaria laevigata (Raf.) Raf.

This interesting plant is parasitic on the roots of white oak trees. It is a perennial, 2—4 feet tall, with smooth stems that are often somewhat purplish. The leaves are lanceolate, 2—4 inches long, with margins that are smooth, or rarely, lobed. Large yellow flowers are borne in a terminal raceme. About 1½ inches long, the tubular corolla becomes 5-lobed near the apex. Individual flower stalks are about ⅛ inch long, smooth, and straight. June—October. Deciduous woods, primarily in the mountains. Ga.—Ala., north to Pa. and Ohio. *Aureolaria pectinata* is distinctive in having glandular hairs on its stems and usually on its leaves. *Aureolaria virginica* has non-glandular hairs on its stems and leaves, hairy capsules, and flower stalks about 1/16 inch long.

Beard-Tongue

Small's Penstemon

Penstemon

Smooth Foxglove

BUTTER-AND-EGGS, TOADFLAX   *Linaria vulgaris* Hill

An herbaceous perennial that spreads rapidly by underground runners as well as by seeds, butter-and-eggs is a well-known weed both in Europe where it is native and in the United States where it has become naturalized. The stems are up to 3 feet high with narrow, linear leaves. Dense terminal racemes of flowers are borne on the numerous upright branches. The pale yellow corolla has a darker yellow or orange palate that extends upward from the lower lip and a tubular spur that extends downward. June—August. Throughout much of North America. *Linaria canadensis* is a slender annual with blue flowers and few or no leaves above the middle of the stem.

MONKEY-FLOWER   *Mimulus ringens* L.

The corolla of this plant somewhat resembles a face, which led to the name *Mimulus*, meaning little mimic. Distinctly square, the stems grow to a height of 2—4 feet from an underground rhizome. The leaves are opposite and sessile. The blue corolla has an erect upper lip, a lower lip that is flared outward and downward, and a yellowish palate that extends upward, closing the corolla tube. A highly variable species, this plant is often separated into several geographical varieties. June—September. Swamps, stream banks, and wet meadows. Ga.—Tex., north to Me. and Kan. *Mimulus alatus* is similar but has leaves that are stalked and stems that are distinctly winged.

BIRD'S-EYE, SPEEDWELL   *Veronica persica* Poir.

A low annual herb with lax stems, bird's-eye has ovate leaves with toothed margins and well-developed petioles. About ½ inch across, the flowers are borne in the axils of upper stem leaves. The bright blue to lavender corolla has darker lines running the length of the petals, and one of the four petals is smaller and lighter than the others. The fruits are heart-shaped and flattened. *Veronica* is a large genus and some of the species are very difficult to distinguish. March—June. Fields, lawns, waste places. Ga.—Tex., north into Can.

CULVER'S-PHYSIC, BOWMAN'S-ROOT   *Veronicastrum virginicum* (L.) Farw.

Veronicastrum is an erect perennial up to 6 feet tall with pointed leaves that are 4—6 inches long and borne in whorls. Cream-white flowers are borne in terminal and axillary racemes 6—10 inches long. The flowers have 5 calyx lobes but only 4 corolla lobes and 2 stamens. Both the stamens and the style are long and protruding, giving the flower cluster a kind of fuzzy appearance. July—August. Woods, meadows, and prairies. Ga.—Tex., north to Mass. and Vt.

Butter-and-Eggs

Monkey-Flower

Culver's-Physic

Bird's-Eye

PURPLE GERARDIA   *Agalinis purpurea* (L.) Pennell

This annual herb is partially parasitic upon the roots of grasses. Profusely branched, the stems are 1—4 feet tall. The leaves are linear, 1—1½ inches long, and rough-hairy on the upper surface. Reddish-purple flowers are borne in open, loose racemes of 6—14 flowers. The corolla tube is 1—1¾ inches long, spreading and 5-lobed at the apex. The throat of the corolla is usually yellow spotted with purple. August—October. Low, wet areas. Ga.—Tex., north to Mass. and Mich. *Agalinis fasciculata* has rough-hairy stems, and leaves borne in small clusters. *Agalinis linifolia* is a perennial with a rhizome and has a corolla with no yellow lines within.

LOUSEWORT   *Pedicularis canadensis* L.

This herbaceous perennial has erect hairy stems, 6—12 inches tall, that are often clustered. Both the basal leaves and the stem leaves are oblong and pinnately divided into many lobes, giving the plant a fernlike appearance. Yellow, or red and yellow, flowers are borne in dense spikes in the axils of leafy bracts. The tubular corolla is 2-lipped, the lower lip 3-lobed and bending downward, the upper lip longer and arching like a beak over the lower lip. Four stamens are found in the upper lip. April-May. Open woods, clearings, and meadows. Fla.—Tex., north into Can.

Bignonia Family   **Bignoniaceae**

CROSS-VINE   *Anisostichus capreolata* (L.) Bureau

Cross-vine is a woody climbing vine with opposite leaves that are divided into two ovate leaflets and a modified leaflet in the form of a branched tendril. Clusters of 2—5 flowers are formed in the axils of stem leaves. About 2 inches long, the bell-shaped, corolla is dull red outside and bright yellow or orange within. The common name is derived from the cross-shaped appearance of the stem in sectional view. April—May. Rich woods and swamps. Fla.—La., north to Md. and Ohio.

TRUMPET-CREEPER, COW-ITCH   *Campsis radicans* (L.) Seemann

One of the most common flowers along fences and roadsides in midsummer, the trumpet-creeper is a woody vine with pinnately compound leaves divided into 10—15 leaflets. Aerial roots serve to anchor the plant as it climbs over fences and other objects. The tubular corolla is about 2 inches long, orange-red outside and yellow within. Contained within the corolla tube are 4 stamens. A spindle-shaped capsule, 4—5 inches long, bears numerous winged seeds. June—August. Fence rows, clearings, and open woods. Fla.—Tex., north to N.J. and Ill.

Purple Gerardia

Lousewort

Cross-Vine

Trumpet-Creeper

Broom-Rape Family   Orobanchaceae

ONE-FLOWERED CANCER-ROOT   *Orobanche uniflora* L.

This small plant grows 2−6 inches tall and is parasitic on the roots of various plants. The stems are white and usually occur in a cluster, with a few overlapping, scalelike leaves at the base of each stem. As the name implies, each stem bears a single, apical flower with a tubular corolla, about an inch long, flaring into 5 rounded lobes. The tube curves slightly downward and is pale lavender with 2 yellow, bearded stripes within. April−May. Moist woods. Fla.−Tex., north into Can.

BEECHDROPS   *Epifagus virginiana* (L.) Bart.

This parasitic plant grows on the roots of beech trees. Purplish-brown or brown stems are 6−18 inches high, have scalelike leaves, and bear racemes of brownish flowers. Less than ½ inch long, the upper flowers are open, 4-lobed, and sterile. The lower flowers that do not open are the only ones that produce fertile seeds. September−November. Rich woods throughout eastern North America.

SQUAWROOT, CANCER-ROOT   *Conopholis americana* (L.) Wallr.

The soft, stout stem of the squawroot is yellow or yellowish-brown with numerous pointed, scalelike leaves overlapping like shingles. At maturity the plants are 4−10 inches tall, and the leaves become dry and hard. Flowers are borne in the axils of the upper scales, and have tubular, 2-lipped corollas, about ½ inch long. The upper lip forms a narrow hood; the lower lip is 3-lobed. The name *Conopholis* means cone scale in reference to the resemblance of the leaves to the scales of pine cones. March−June. Dry woods, parasitic on oak roots. Ga.−Ala., north to Mass. and Wis.

Bladderwort Family   Lentibulariaceae

YELLOW BUTTERWORT   *Pinguicula lutea* Walt.

Yellow butterwort is a small, insectivorous perennial that grows 4−12 inches tall. The yellowish-green leaves, in a basal rosette, are sticky or greasy to the touch and have the edges rolled up forming a point toward the tip. When small insects are caught in this sticky surface, the edges of the leaf curl over still further, covering the insect. Enzymes are then secreted which digest the insect. Solitary yellow flowers, about an inch long, are borne on leafless stalks 5−20 inches tall. The 2-lipped corolla has a conspicuous spur on the back side. February−May. Moist, sandy soil, low pinelands. Coastal Plain. Fla., Ala., Miss., N.C.

One-flowered Cancer-Root

Squawroot

Beechdrops

Yellow Butterwort

BLUE BUTTERWORT   *Pinguicula caerulea* Walt.

Pinguicula caerulea has a leafless flowering stalk, about 6 inches high, that is densely hairy toward the base. On both the stem and the leaves are glandular hairs. The flowers are about an inch across with a blue to violet corolla bearing a hollow spur less than ½ inch long. April—May. Low pinelands on the Coastal Plain. Ala.—Fla., north to N. C.

SMALL BUTTERWORT   *Pinguicula pumila* Michx.

The smallest of the butterworts in Alabama, this plant has a flowering stem only 3—4 inches tall. The basal rosette of leaves is about an inch across with each leaf less than ½ inch wide. The small flowers are less than an inch long. Varying in color from blue to pale lavender to almost white, usually with some yellow within the tube, the corolla has a spur about ⅛ inch long. April—May. Low pinelands on the Coastal Plain. Ala.—Fla., north to N. C.

FLOATING BLADDERWORT   *Utricularia inflata* Walt.

The bladderwort is a small, carnivorous, aquatic plant with a stem 4—10 inches high, rising from a whorl of pinnately divided leaves. The leaves have inflated stalks known as floats, and the lower, submersed leaves branch into many hairlike segments bearing numerous small, bladderlike traps. Tiny insects are swept into the bladders and held by a trap-door mechanism. There are several species of bladderworts in Alabama. *Utricularia inflata* can be distinguished by its inflated leaf stalks and its yellow flowers, about ¾ inch across. May—November. Ponds, ditches. Fla.—Tex., north to Me. A terrestrial species, *U. subulata,* has yellow flowers and tiny leaves that are not dissected; *U. purpurea* has purple flowers, and leaves without inflated stalks.

Acanthus Family   **Acanthaceae**

WILD PETUNIA   *Ruellia strepens* L.

Wild petunia is an erect perennial, 1—4 feet tall, often finely downy on the stems and leaves. The leaves are opposite and ovate with pointed tips. Pale bluish-purple flowers are borne singly or in pairs, subtended by 2 small leaves or bracts. Up to 2 inches long, the trumpet-shaped corolla has 5 widely flaring lobes. Lance-shaped lobes from the calyx tube are also distinctive in this species. May—September. Woods, thickets, often in calcareous soil. Ga.—Tex., north to N. J. and Ill.

Blue Butterwort

Small Butterwort

Floating Bladderwort

Wild Petunia

LOW WILD PETUNIA   *Ruellia humilis* Nutt.

An extremely variable species, *Ruellia humilis* is difficult to distinguish from several closely related plants that also occur in Alabama. Generally, this species is hairy with a branched stem 1–2 feet tall. The leaves are opposite and sessile, usually oblong to ovate. Bluish-purple flowers, about 1½ inches long, may be either solitary or in crowded clusters in the axils of upper leaves. May—September. Open woods, prairies, sandy soil. Fla.—Tex., north to Pa. and Ind. Two related species are *R. ciliosa*, having petioled leaves in a basal rosette, and *R. caroliniensis* having petioled leaves but without a basal rosette.

WATER WILLOW   *Justicia americana* (L.) Vahl.

Water willow is an aquatic perennial that grows to a height of 3 feet above the water, spreading and forming colonies by means of rhizomes. The linear leaves, 3–6 inches long, are similar to those of willows, which led to the inappropriate common name. The flowers are white to pale violet, marked with purple. Tubular at the base, the corolla is 2-lipped above, with the upper lip arching upward and the lower lip 3-lobed and spreading. There are only 2 stamens. June—October. Shallow water along lakes and streams. Ga.—Tex., north into Can.

Madder Family   Rubiaceae

BUTTONBUSH   *Cephalanthus occidentalis* L.

Growing to a height of 5–10 feet, this shrub has opposite or whorled leaves 2–6 inches long. Dense, ball-shaped clusters of flowers about an inch in diameter are produced on the ends of branches and in the axils of leaves. An individual flower has a white, tubular corolla, less than ½ inch long, with 4 stamens inserted on the rim of the tube and protruding. June—August. Low, wet areas along ponds and streams. Fla.—Mex., north into Can.

PARTRIDGE-BERRY   *Mitchella repens* L.

Partridge-berry is a trailing, evergreen perennial with stems that root at the nodes and often form a dense mat. The shining, somewhat leathery leaves are rounded or elliptic, and are ½–1 inch long. Fragrant white flowers are borne in pairs in the axil of each leaf. The corolla is funnel-shaped, hairy on the inside, and has 4 short, spreading lobes. Formed by a fusion of the 2 ovaries of the twin flowers, the fruit is a globular scarlet berry that is edible and persists throughout the winter. Late May—July. Rich woods. Fla.—Tex., north into Can.

Low Wild Petunia

Water Willow

Buttonbush

Partridge-Berry

SMALL BLUETS, INNOCENCE   *Houstonia pusilla* Schoepf

A small, solitary annual, usually 2—4 inches tall, this plant has basal leaves that are spatulate, about ¼—½ inch long and stem leaves that are narrow and much smaller. The corolla is deep blue-purple with a yellow throat, about ¼—⅜ inch across. March—April. Open woods, fields, meadows. Ga.—Tex., north to Va. and Mo. *Houstonia caerulea* is tufted perennial with a pale blue corolla with a yellow center. In this species the flowers have either a long protruding style or a short style that is below the anthers. Fertile seeds are produced only by cross-pollination between plants with different style lengths.

PURPLE BLUETS   *Houstonia purpurea* L.

This is a many-stemmed perennial, 4—16 inches tall. The leaves are opposite, sessile, ovate, and about 1½ inches long. Purple to white in color, the funnel-shaped corollas are hairy within. April—July. Open woods, rocky slopes, and meadows. Ga.—La., north to Pa. and Ia. *Houstonia tenuifolia* has narrowly linear leaves and stalked flowers; *H. nigricans* has narrowly linear leaves and mostly sessile flowers.

PYGMY BLUETS   *Houstonia pygmaea* Muel. & Muel.

Pygmy bluets are very low-growing plants, usually only 2—3 inches tall. They are easily distinguished from other bluets by their pale rose-lavender petals with greenish-yellow throats. The lobes of the corolla are ovate and abruptly pointed at the apex. Otherwise, this species is similar to *Houstonia pusilla*—the lilac-colored flower shown with *H. pygmaea* in the photograph at right. April—May. This is a Western species, recently discovered invading lawns and meadows in central Alabama. Formerly it had not been recorded east of Texas.

Honeysuckle Family   Caprifoliaceae

CORAL HONEYSUCKLE, TRUMPET HONEYSUCKLE   *Lonicera sempervirens* L.

Coral honeysuckle is a climbing vine with smooth stems and leaves. The elliptic or ovate leaves are opposite, with the pair just beneath the inflorescence usually fused laterally. Borne at the end of new growth, the flower cluster contains several groups of 3 flowers. The tubular corolla is about 1½—2 inches long, red on the outside and occasionally yellow within. The lobes of the corolla have fine hairs on the inner surface. Often cultivated around suburban mailboxes, this beautiful native species is sometimes referred to as "mailbox honeysuckle." March—June. Woods and thickets. Fla.—Tex., north to Me. and Ia.

Small Bluets

Purple Bluets

Pygmy Bluets

Coral Honeysuckle

Bluebell Family   Campanulaceae

VENUS'S-LOOKING-GLASS   *Specularia perfoliata* (L.) A. DC.

Venus's-looking-glass is a slender, erect plant that usually has a simple, angled stem, 6—18 inches high. The leaves are alternate, rounded or heart-shaped, sessile, and clasping. Borne sessile in the axils of upper stem leaves, the purple flowers are about ½ inch across, deeply 5-lobed, and tubular at the extreme base only. Some of the lower flowers never open but develop fertile seeds by self-pollination. April—June. Roadsides, fields, and gardens. Fla.—Tex., north to Me. and Mich. A closely related species, *Specularia biflora*, has ovate leaves that do not clasp the stem.

AMERICAN BELLFLOWER   *Campanula americana* L.

This tall erect biennial has a simple or branched stem up to 6 feet tall. The alternate leaves are thick, lanceolate, toothed, and 3—6 inches long. The flowers are borne in a long spike, with the lower flowers in the axils of leaves, and the upper ones in the axils of bracts. Blue with a pale ring at the throat, the corolla is ¾ inch across, and has a protruding and curved style about an inch long. The flowers of this species are not bell-shaped. June—September. Moist woods, thickets, and roadsides. Ga.—Miss., north to Can.

SOUTHERN HAREBELL   *Campanula divaricata* Michx.

A smooth-stemmed, loosely-branched perennial, 1—3 feet tall, Southern harebell has thin, lanceolate leaves 1—4 inches long. The inflorescence is compound and lax, bearing numerous, drooping flowers. The pale-blue Bell-shaped corolla is about ⅓ inch long and has 5 recurved, shallow lobes. The style is usually straight and extends about ⅓ inch from the corolla tube. July—October. Dry woods, rocky slopes, cliffs. Ga.—Ala., north to Va. and Ky.

CARDINAL FLOWER   *Lobelia cardinalis* L.

A slender spike of brilliant scarlet flowers is the outstanding feature of this tall perennial. Growing 2—4 feet tall, simple stems bear alternate, lanceolate, toothed leaves. The corolla is 1—2 inches long and 2-lipped, with the upper lip divided into 2 erect lobes, and the lower lip 3-lobed and spreading. Five stamens are joined around the style, forming a curved column that protrudes from the corolla. July—October. Stream banks, swamps, and low wet places. Ga.—Tex., north to Can.

Venus's-Looking-Glass

American Bellflower

Southern Harebell

Cardinal Flower

GREAT BLUE LOBELIA   *Lobelia siphilitica* L.

The great blue lobelia is a tall handsome perennial, 2—5 feet tall, and has alternate leaves that are lanceolate and toothed. Borne in dense terminal spikes, the numerous flowers are light or dark blue, with tubular, 2-lipped corollas. The upper lip is erect and 2-lobed; the lower lip is 3-lobed and marked with white. The lower side of the corolla tube has several darker blue stripes about an inch long. July—October. Damp ground, stream banks, and roadside ditches. Ga.—La., north to Can. *Lobelia amoena* has elliptic leaves, and spikes with the flowers borne primarily on one side.

Sunflower Family   Asteraceae

CHICORY, BLUE SAILORS   *Cichorium intybus* L.

An introduced species from Europe, chicory has become very weedy but is attractive. The plants reach a height of 4—5 feet and have oblong leaves that are toothed, sessile, and often clasping. Numerous blue, pink, or rarely, white flower heads are sessile along the stem. The heads are 1—2 inches across and consist entirely of petallike ray flowers that are 5-lobed at the apex. The roots of chicory are sometimes used to flavor coffee. May—October. Fields, roadsides, waste places, thoughout much of North America.

INDIAN PLANTAIN   *Cacalia tuberosa* Nutt.

Indian plantain is a large plant, 2—6 feet high, with long-petioled, elliptic leaves at the base. The stem is smooth, angled, and grooved. Clustered at the apex of the stem, numerous dense flower heads about an inch long bear greenish or white disc flowers. June—August. Prairies, damp fields, bogs. Ala.—Tex., north to Ont. and Minn. Great Indian plantain, *Cacalia muhlenbergii* has green stems tinged with purple, and kidney-shaped leaves; *C. lanceolata* has narrow, lanceolate leaves about ½ inch wide.

DWARF DANDELION   *Krigia virginica* (L.) Willd.

Dwarf dandelion is a slender annual, 2—12 inches high, with leaves only at the base. The leaves are linear to elliptic, 1—4 inches long, and often variously toothed or lobed. Heads of yellow or orange ray flowers are borne on naked stems and subtended by 9—18 clustered bracts. The rays are about ½ inch long with a pappus (calyx) of 5—7 slender scales alternating with bristles. March—June. Woods, fields, and roadsides. Fla.—Tex., north to N. J. and Mo. *Krigia dandelion* is similar but is a perennial with small tubers on its roots.

Great Blue Lobelia

Chicory

Indian Plantain

Dwarf Dandelion

RED-SEEDED DANDELION   *Taraxacum erythrospermum* Andrz. ex Besser

Native to the Old World, this dandelion is now naturalized over most of eastern North America, especially on lawns. It is a perennial with a large taproot from which a rosette of leaves forms. The leaves are 4—8 inches long, deeply cut into sharp-pointed segments. Consisting of ray flowers only, the flower heads are 1—1½ inches across, The fruits are reddish-brown with an umbrellalike pappus of capillary bristles. March—June. Lawns, fields, open areas, throughout eastern North America. *Taraxacum officinale*, a similar and even more widely distributed species can be distinguished by its greenish fruits. When young, the leaves of both species are edible.

TWO-COLORED THISTLE   *Carduus discolor* (Muhl. ex. Willd.) Nutt.

This thistle is a robust biennial 3—10 feet high with deeply-cleft leaves that are woolly on the underside. The flower heads are purple, 1—1½ inches across, surrounded by clustered bracts with spines that bend out from the head. There is also an inner layer of spineless bracts. White and feathery, the pappus is about an inch long. July—October. Woods, thickets, pastures, and prairies. Ga.—Miss. and Mo., north into Can. *Carduus spinosissimus* is easily distinguished by its yellow flowering heads.

SOW THISTLE   *Sonchus asper* (L.) Hill

Sow thistle is a rather unattractive winter annual with fleshy stems, 1—3 feet tall, and spiny-margined, clasping leaves. When cut, the stems and leaves yield a milky latex. The flowering heads are about ½ inch long and an inch across when open, and consist of pale yellow ray flowers only. The fruits are reddish-brown, with a pappus of white capillary bristles. March—July. Roadsides, fields, and waste places. Throughout the U.S. and into Can.

QUEEN-OF-THE-MEADOW   *Vernonia gigantea* (Walt.) Trel.

A coarse, widely-branched perennial 3-8 feet tall, queen-of-the-meadow has elliptic leaves that are sharply pointed and 4—8 inches long. In dense flat-topped clusters at the ends of branches, the flower heads contain disc flowers only and usually 12 or fewer of these per head. The bracts surrounding the heads have purple tips, and the pappus is purple. May—November. Low ground, swamps, river bottoms. Ga. and Ala. *Vernonia noveboracensis* can be distinguished by having heads with 30—50 flowers. A smaller species, 2—4 feet tall, *V. angustifolia* has very narrow, rough-hairy leaves.

Red-seeded Dandelion

Two-colored Thistle

Sow Thistle

Queen-of-the-Meadow

SUNBONNET   *Chaptalia tomentosa* Vent.

The characteristic angle of the flower head or "bonnet" gives a coy appearance to this perennial known as sunbonnet. In a basal rosette, the leaves are densely white-hairy beneath and 2—5 inches long. The naked stem is 6—12 inches tall, bearing a single nodding flower head about an inch across. The ray flowers are white, often with some purple on the back, and the disc flowers are yellow to cream-colored. The flowers close at night, then open the following morning and turn toward the sun. March—May. Pine barrens, savannas, and sandhills. Coastal Plain. N.C.—Fla., west to Tex.

BLAZING STAR   *Liatris squarrosa* (L.) Michx.

A perennial with a stem growing 1—3 feet tall from a rounded corm, *Liatris squarrosa* has stiff, linear leaves, the lower ones up to a foot or more long and those up the stem much smaller. Heads of purple disc flowers about an inch across contain 20—40 flowers. The surrounding bracts are spreading and have sharp, stiff points. The pappus is feathery. Late June—August. Upland woods and fields. Ga.—Tex., north to Del. and Ill.

BLAZING STAR   *Liatris scariosa* (L.) Willd.

This perennial has a stem that is 1—5 feet tall and mostly downy and unbranched. The lower leaves are up to 2 inches wide and a foot long; the upper leaves become progressively reduced and linear. Purple disc flowers are borne in round, stalked heads of 25—60 flowers. Surrounding the heads are thick, rounded bracts that are green, often with purple margins. The pappus is less than ½ inch long and consists of barbed bristles. August—September. Dry woodlands. Ga.—Miss., north to Pa. and W. Va.

BLAZING STAR   *Liatris tenuifolia* Nutt.

This blazing star is a perennial herb with smooth stems 2—6 feet tall. The linear to threadlike leaves of the lower stem are up to 6 inches long, but the upper leaves are so small that the flowering stem appears leafless toward the top. Usually 5-flowered, the heads of violet disc flowers occur in tall, thin spikes. The bracts surrounding the heads usually have pink, translucent margins. Late August—October. Pine barrens and open woods. Coastal Plain. Ala.—Fla., north to N.C.

Sunbonnet

Liatris squarrosa

Liatris scariosa

Liatris tenuifolia

BLAZING STAR
Liatris provincialis Godfrey

This rare species has smooth, flexible stems with many leaves near the base. The leaves are glabrous and linear, 1—3 inches long. Borne in terminal spikes, the flower heads stand at right angles to the stem. The heads, containing only disc flowers, are lavender and few-flowered. July—October. Pinelands, sandy soil. Rare. Fla.—Ala.

GRASS-LEAVED LIATRIS
Liatris graminifolia Willd.

Growing up to 5 feet tall, *Liatris graminifolia* is a smooth-stemmed perennial and has linear leaves 2—8 inches long. The flower heads have 10—12 lavender disc flowers surrounded by green bracts with blunt tips. About ⅛ inch long, the corolla tube is hairy within. The pappus consists of tawny capillary bristles. September—October. Open woods and old fields. Ala.—Ga., north to N.J.

FALSE LIATRIS
Carphephorus pseudo-liatris (Nutt.) T. & G.

Very similar to *Liatris*, *Carphephorus* is distinguished primarily by having the flowering heads in flat-topped clusters rather than in spikes or racemes. False liatris has unbranched, hairy stems, 1—3 feet tall with long, needlelike basal leaves. The leaves up the stem become very small, those above the middle of the stem almost scalelike. The heads contain only disc flowers, these being rose-purple and enclosed by broadly linear bracts. The pappus consists of pale bristles with small, backward-pointing barbs. August—October. Moist pinelands on the Coastal Plain. Ga., Fla.—La.

VANILLA PLANT, DEER'S TONGUE
Trilisa odoratissima (Walt. ex. Gmel.) Cass.

Vanilla plant is an herbaceous perennial, 2—6 feet tall, and has a distinct odor of vanilla when drying. The plant has fleshy roots and a woody crown, producing one or more stems each year. Thick and leathery, the basal leaves are up to a foot long. The stem leaves are much smaller and are reduced up the stem. The flower heads are borne in large, flat-topped clusters with lateral branches that are usually taller than the central cluster. Lavender to pink in color, the flowers are all disc flowers and have a pappus of barbed bristles. This species is collected for the extraction of coumarin, used in making artificial vanilla. July—October. Pine barrens, savannas, and sandy woods. Coastal Plain. Fla.—La., north to N.C.

Blazing Star

Grass-leaved Liatris

False Liatris

Vanilla Plant

185

MISTFLOWER, WILD AGERATUM — *Eupatorium coelestinum* L.

This branched perennial, 1—3 feet tall, is very similar to the cultivated ageratum. The stems are usually in clumps and are greenish-purple. Borne in pairs, the triangular leaves have rounded teeth and wrinkled surfaces. Many-flowered heads of pale blue, or rarely, white flowers are borne in clusters at the ends of branches. Each head is about ¼ inch across, containing 40—50 disc flowers with thread-shaped styles that are about twice as long as the corollas. The pappus consists of white capillary bristles. July—October. Moist woods, meadows, and stream banks. Fla.—Tex., north to NJ. and Kan.

SWEET JOE-PYE WEED — *Eupatorium purpureum* L.

Sweet Joe-pye weed is a fibrous-rooted perennial, 2—6 feet tall with leaves in whorls of 3—5. The lanceolate leaves are up to 8 inches long and have sharply-toothed margins. When bruised or dried, the leaves and stems have a strong vanilla fragrance. In large-branched, round-topped clusters at the top of the stem are numerous flower heads, having 3—7 disc flowers with cream-white to pinkish corollas. July—October. N. Fla.—Okla., north to N.H. and Neb.

BONESET, THOROUGHWORT — *Eupatorium perfoliatum* L.

This boneset is a rough, hairy perennial, 2—6 feet tall. The opposite leaves are perfoliate, that is, with the bases joined around the stem so that the stem seems to go through the leaves. The common name thoroughwort was likely derived from "throughwort," in reference to the perfoliate leaves. The dense heads of 7—15 dull white flowers are crowded into numerous clusters of 25—30 heads at the top of the stem. Boneset tea, made from the dried leaves, was used extensively in the past as a tonic for a variety of ills. August—October. Moist or wet woods, meadows, and bogs. Fla.—Tex., north into Can.

WHITE SNAKEROOT — *Eupatorium rugosum* Houtt.

This fibrous-rooted, woodland perennial is 1—5 feet tall, usually with the stems in clumps. The thin, smooth, opposite leaves are long-petioled, and have blades up to 4 inches long. In open branching panicles, the flower heads are about ¼ inch long with 12—24 white disc flowers in each. This plant is poisonous to cattle, and the toxic substance is transmitted in milk, causing "milk sickness". Late July—October. Rich woods, fields, and disturbed sites. N. Fla.—Tex., north to Can.

Mistflower

Sweet Joe-Pye Weed

Boneset

White Snakeroot

CLIMBING HEMPWEED   *Mikania scandens* (L.) Willd.

The climbing hempweed is an herbaceous vine with 4-angled stems up to 10 feet long. Usually triangular, the leaves are opposite and 2—4 inches long. Flower heads each contain 4 disc flowers with white or pink corollas, surrounded by 4 bracts. The pappus consists of short, white, barbed bristles. July—October. Woods, thickets, and marshes, usually in very wet areas. Fla.—Tex., north to Me. and S. Ont.

DAISY FLEABANE   *Erigeron philadelphicus* L.

This fleabane is a perennial, 1—3 feet high, with a hairy stem and basal leaves that have short, winged petioles. The smaller stem leaves, usually 2—3 inches long, are sessile and at the base have earlike lobes that clasp the stem. The heads are about ½ inch across consisting of numerous flowers, of which the rays are white to pinkish and the discs are yellow. April—June. Rich thickets, meadows, and disturbed sites. Fla.—Tex., north into Can. *Erigeron pulchellus* is distinguished by having stolons and about half as many (50) ray flowers; *E. strigosus* has narrow stem leaves that are not clasping; *E. annuus* has wider leaves, usually ½ inch or more, that are hairy beneath.

WHITE DAISY, LAZY DAISY   *Aphanostephus skirrobasis* (DC.) Trel.

White daisy is a bushy annual, about a foot tall, that resembles an aster. The alternate, oblong leaves are about an inch long and have smooth margins. About ½—1 inch across, the solitary heads bear numerous disc and ray flowers. The ray flowers vary from white to violet and the disc flowers are yellow. The pappus consists of a smooth or toothed crown of scales. April—July. Dry, sandy soil. Coastal Plain. Fla.—Tex. and Kan.

STIFF ASTER   *Aster paludosus* Ait.

There are numerous species of *Aster* occurring in Alabama. The three mentioned here serve only as an introduction to this complex group. Stiff aster is a perennial with a smooth or slightly hairy stem, 1—2 feet tall. The leaves are linear to elliptic, less than ½ inch wide, and 3—6 inches long. Flower heads, 1½—2 inches across, are borne in sparse clusters of 1—9 heads near the top of the stem. Both ray and disc flowers are present, each head containing 20—30 deep blue to violet rays about ½ inch long. The pappus consists of capillary bristles. July—October. Savannas and sandhills. Ala.—N.C.

Climbing Hempweed

Daisy Fleabane

White Daisy

Stiff Aster

STIFF-LEAVED ASTER, BRISTLE-LEAVED ASTER   *Aster linariifolius* L.

This perennial species usually forms clumps with few to many rigid stems, 1—2 feet tall. The stiff, needlelike leaves are ½—1 inch long. The flower heads are 1—1½ inches across with 7—15 blue to violet rays. September—November. Dry woods and clearings. N. Fla.—Tex., north to N.B. and Minn. *Aster ericoides* is another common species with narrow, stiff leaves. It can be distinguished by its cluster of bracts that are spine-tipped and green.

GIANT GOLDENROD   *Solidago gigantea* Ait.

Solidago is another large and complex genus with species that are difficult to distinguish even by professionals. The following five species will serve only as an introduction to the species in Alabama. Giant goldenrod has stems up to 9 feet tall, usually covered with a whitish powder. The thin, lanceolate leaves are sharply toothed above the middle and clearly 3-nerved. Borne in dense panicles with the flowering branches recurving at the tips, the heads contain few ray flowers and numerous disc flowers. The pappus consists of capillary bristles. July—October. Low woods, old fields, and stream banks. Fla.—Tex., and Ore., north into Can.

COMMON GOLDENROD   *Solidago altissima* L.

Common goldenrod is another tall species, 3—8 feet high, and the entire plant is covered with stiff grayish hairs that are rough to the touch. The lanceolate leaves are 3—4 inches long and prominently 3-nerved. Distinctly pyramidal in outline, the panicle of flower heads consists of numerous slender heads about ⅛ inch long with 12—18 flowers. This is probably the most common species of goldenrod in the state. September—October. Old fields, pastures, and disturbed sites. Fla.—Tex., north into Can.

SILVERROD, WHITE GOLDENROD   *Solidago bicolor* L.

Silverrod is easily distinguished from other goldenrods in the state by its white ray flowers. The stems are 2—5 feet tall and covered with fine, downlike hairs. The elliptic leaves are 2—5 inches long and about an inch wide, with the two lateral veins obscure. Clustered in narrow panicles, the heads bear 10—20 flowers. September—October. Woodlands and roadsides. Ga.—Mo., north into Can.

Stiff-leaved Aster

Giant Goldenrod

Common Goldenrod

Silverrod

SHARP-TOOTHED GOLDENROD   *Solidago arguta* Ait.

Solidago arguta has erect, usually solitary stems that are 3—6 feet tall. The basal leaves are up to 7 inches long, rapidly reduced up the stem to half that size. The margins are sharply double-toothed and a pair of lateral veins is distinct. The heads have 10—20 flowers in panicles, with the flowers borne mostly on one side of each flowering stem. July—October. Woodlands, old fields, and roadsides. Ala.—Ga., north to Me. and Ill.

GRASS-LEAVED GOLDENROD   *Solidago graminifolia* (L.) Salisb.

This is a highly variable species with several geographical varieties across North America. Usually hairy, the angular stems are 1—4 feet tall, growing from a long, slender rhizome. Smooth, narrow, and grasslike, the leaves have 2—4 prominent lateral veins. Flower heads of 12—45 flowers are borne in dense clusters. The rays are short, 1/16—1/8 inch long. August—September. Open ground and roadsides. Ala.—Mo., north into Can. and S.D.

HAIRY GOLDEN ASTER   *Heterotheca pilosa* (Nutt.) Shin.

Despite the deceptive common name, this plant is not a true aster. *Heterotheca pilosa* is an annual with erect stems that are 1—4 feet tall and covered with long, sticky hairs. The leaves are sessile and sometimes clasping. The heads are about an inch across with numerous yellow disc flowers and 12—24 yellow ray flowers. The pappus consists of an outer row of short, scalelike bristles, and an inner row of long bristles. June— October. Sandy fields. Fla.—Tex., north to N.C., Mo. and Kan. *Heterotheca subaxillaris* is distinctive in having disc flowers that develop flat fruits with a pappus, and ray flowers that develop thick, angled fruits without a pappus.

GOLDEN ASTER   *Heterotheca mariana* (L.) Shin.

This perennial usually occurs in clumps with several stems arising from a short rhizome. When young, the stems and leaves are woolly, becoming less so with age. The basal leaves are elliptic, 2—5 inches long; those borne up the stem are similar in shape and usually smaller. The heads have 12—25 ray flowers almost an inch long and numerous disc flowers. The bracts surrounding the heads are covered with stalked glands. June—October. Dry sandy woods and old fields. Fla.—Tex., north to N.Y. and Ohio.

Sharp-toothed Goldenrod

Grass-leaved Goldenrod

Hairy Golden Aster

Golden Aster

CUP PLANT, INDIAN CUP
Silphium perfoliatum L.

The cup plant is easy to identify by its distinctive leaves that are joined around the stem forming small cups. The stem is 4-angled, 3—8 feet tall, bearing leaves that are 4—12 inches long and rough to the touch. The lower leaves have petioles and do not form the cups. Open clusters of flower heads are borne near the top of the stem. Numerous ray and disc flowers are in each head, but only the ray flowers are fertile. June—August. Low meadows, wet woods, and marshes. Ga.—Okla., north into Can.

ROSINWEED, SILPHIUM
Silphium integrifolium Michx.

This silphium is distinctive in having leaves with smooth margins. The stems are round, smooth, 2—6 feet tall and bear leaves that are opposite and very rough to the touch. The yellow heads consist of 15—24 fertile ray flowers about an inch long, surrounding numerous sterile disc flowers. The fruits are winged. July—September. Prairies and sandy woodlands. Ala.—Tex., north to Ill. and Wis. *Silphium laciniatum* has leaves that are deeply cut and seem to stand at right angles to the stem, pointing north and south. For this reason it is often called compass plant.

PURPLE CONEFLOWER
Echinacea purpurea (L.) Moench

The purple coneflower is a perennial with thick, fleshy roots, and stems up to 4 feet high. The leaves are rough-hairy to almost spiny, clustered in a basal rosette and on the lower part of the stem. Flower heads are solitary, 2—3 inches across, with 12—20 ray flowers surrounding a dome-shaped cluster of disc flowers. The bracts of the disc flowers are spiny and extend above the flowers. June—August. Woodlands and roadsides. Ga.—La., north to Va. and Mich. *Echinacea laevigata* has smooth stems and leaves, and ray flowers 2—3 inches long; *E. pallida* has rough-hairy leaves that are narrow, tapering, and mostly basal.

BLACK-EYED SUSAN
Rudbeckia hirta L.

The familiar black-eyed Susan is usually perennial but often functions as an annual, flowering the first year from seeds. Usually several stems, 1—3 feet high, arise from a central crown and bear elliptic to lanceolate leaves that are rough-hairy. The flower heads are terminal, 1—2 inches across, with 8—20 sterile yellow ray flowers and a dense mound of fertile dark purple or brown disc flowers. The fruits are 4-angled, and there is no pappus. May—July. Fields, meadows, and roadsides. Ga.—Tex., north to Mass. and Ill.

Cup Plant

Purple Coneflower

Rosinweed

Black-eyed Susan

GREEN CONEFLOWER   *Rudbeckia laciniata* L.

Green coneflower is easily distinguished by its greenish-yellow disc flowers in contrast to the purplish-brown disc flowers of other coneflowers and black-eyed Susans in the state. It also has smooth stems, 3—8 inches high, growing from a rhizome. Deeply lobed or toothed, the leaves usually have the lobes extending nearly to the midrib. The ray flowers are yellow, reflexed, and 1—1½ inches long. July—October. Wet fields, woodlands, and stream banks. Fla.—La., north to Can.

CONEFLOWER   *Dracopis amplexicaulis* (Vahl.) Cass.

This coneflower is an annual with smooth stems 1—3 feet tall. The leaves are oblong with a heart-shaped, clasping base. The brownish-olive disc flowers form a columnar mound ½—1¼ inch long. About an inch long, the ray flowers are yellow with a brown base. This species can be distinguished from related ones by the chafflike bract at the base of each ray flower. May—June. Prairies, waste ground, roadsides. Ga.—Tex., north to Mo. and Kan.

NARROW-LEAVED SUNFLOWER   *Helianthus angustifolius* L.

There are numerous species of sunflowers in Alabama, and many of them are difficult to distinguish. One of the most beautiful, distinctive, and widespread species is the narrow-leaved sunflower. It has rough-hairy stems, up to 7 feet tall, bearing alternate leaves about 4—6 inches long and ¼ inch wide. The surfaces of the leaves are rough, and the margins are inrolled. The flower heads are about 2 inches across, with dark purple-brown disc flowers and yellow ray flowers. These plants usually occur in dense clumps and are spectacular along roadsides in early fall. August—October. Moist ground, pine barrens, and roadsides. Fla.—Tex., north to N.J. and s. Ind.

PINK COREOPSIS   *Coreopsis nudata* Nutt.

Pink coreopsis is easily distinguished by long, narrow leaves that are round in cross section. The stems are 2—4 feet high, bearing very few leaves. Borne on the ends of branches, the flower heads are about an inch across. The ray flowers are pinkish-purple on the outside, often becoming whitish within; the discs are usually slightly darker than the rays. May—June. Wet pinelands and cypress swamps. Fla., Ga., and Ala.

Green Coneflower

Coneflower

Narrow-leaved Sunflower

Pink Coreopsis

EARED COREOPSIS   *Coreopsis auriculata* L.

The eared coreopsis derives its name from the two earlike lobes at the base of the leaves. The plant is stoloniferous, forming small colonies that reach a height of 2 feet. The flowering heads, about 1½–2 inches across, are borne on long stalks and have orange-yellow disc and ray flowers. The rays are toothed at the apex. April–June. Woodlands, often in calcareous soil. Fla.–La., north to Va. and Ky.

WHORLED TICKSEED   *Coreopsis major* Walt.

Whorled tickseed is so named because encircling the stem at intervals are whorls of sessile leaves. Each leaf is divided into 3 narrow, lance-shaped segments. Reaching a height of 1–3 feet, the plant is a perennial with a long slender rhizome. The flower heads are 1–2 inches across with yellow ray flowers and red or yellow disc flowers. The rays are not conspicuously toothed. May–August. Woodlands, thickets, and old fields. Fla.–Miss., north to Va. and W. Va.

CALLIOPSIS   *Coreopsis tinctoria* Nutt.

This smooth annual is 2–4 feet high with basal leaves that are pinnately divided into very narrow segments and upper stem leaves that are opposite and petioled but not divided. About an inch across, the numerous flowering heads are surrounded by 1–2 series of bracts and have dark purple-brown disc flowers and ray flowers that are golden yellow with a purple-brown base. Rarely, the ray flowers may be all yellow or all purple-brown. May–July. A Western species, becoming widespread in the East. Ala–La., west to Ariz. and Cal., north into Can.

BARBARA'S-BUTTONS   *Marshallia trinervia* (Walt.) Trel. ex Branner and Cov.

A perennial with a solitary stem 1–2 feet tall, growing from a creeping rhizome, this plant has thin, 3-nerved leaves about 4 inches long. The flower heads are pink or purple and contain only disc flowers. The corolla tube is about ¼ inch long. The pappus consists of 5–6 membranaceous scales. July. Pinelands and damp woods. Ala–Miss., north to Va. and Tenn. *Marshallia obovata* has longer leaves, with leaves occurring only on the lower half of the stem.

Eared Coreopsis

Whorled Tickseed

Barbara's-Buttons

Calliopsis

GAILLARDIA
Gaillardia pulchella Foug.

Gaillardia is an annual or a short-lived perennial herb with hairy stems that grow to a height of 1—2 feet. Usually branching from the base, it bears linear-elliptic leaves. The flowering heads have greenish-yellow discs with purplish corolla lobes, and purple rays, often with yellow or white tips. The pappus consists of membranaceous scales. April—November. Sandy fields, beaches, and roadsides. Fla.—Ariz., north to N.Y. *Gaillardia aestivalis* is similar, but the ray flowers rarely develop, and the disc flowers are purplish-red.

SNEEZEWEED, BITTERWEED
Helenium autumnale L.

This weedy species is a branched perennial with one to several stems arising from a single crown. The stems are 1—5 feet tall and appear to be winged due to the bases of leaves that extend down the stem. The basal leaves are elliptic, 3—7 inches long; those above are greatly reduced. Flowering heads are 1—2 inches across with yellow disc and ray flowers, the ray flowers being 3-lobed at the apex. The pappus consists of papery scales with an awnlike appendage. May—August. Pastures, meadows, and ditches. Fla.—Tex., north to Md. and Mo.

YARROW, MILFOIL
Achillea millefolium L.

Yarrow is a common weed growing to a height of 1—2 feet, with leaves finely cut into numerous threadlike divisions. The flowering heads are in terminal clusters, with each each head only about ¼ inch across. The ray flowers are white and only the pistil is functional. The white disc flowers contain both sexes, but no pappus is present. April—november. Fields and waste places, throughout eastern North America.

OXEYE DAISY, WHITE DAISY
Chrysanthemum leucanthemum L.

Oxeye daisy is a beautiful perennial, 2—3 feet tall, often locally abundant, covering fields or roadsides. The basal leaves are spatulate with long petioles, the upper stem leaves are more oblong and have short petioles or are sessile. The flowering heads are 1½—2 inches across with golden yellow disc flowers and white ray flowers. The name *leucanthemum* means white flower. May—July. Fields, roadsides, waste places. Ala.—Ga., north into Can.

Gaillardia

Sneezeweed

Yarrow

Oxeye Daisy

PHOTOGRAPHIC CREDITS

Listed below are the photographers with the scientific names of the plants they photographed. Only the generic name is listed unless more than one species is included in the book.

Amy Mason:
Achillea, Actaea, Agalinis, Amianthium, Amsonia, Anemone quinquefolia, Apios, Aplectrum, Aquilegia, Argemone, Arisaema, Aristolochia macrophylla, Asarum, Asclepias amplexicaulis, A. humistrata, A. lanceolata, A. variegata, A. verticillata, Asclepiodora, Aster paludosus, Aureolaria, Blephilia, Cacalia, Callirhoë, Calycanthus, Calystegia, Camassia, Campanula divaricata, Carphephorus, Cassia, Ceanothus, Chelone, Cichorium, Cimicifuga, Cleistes, Clematis viorna, Clitoria, Cnidoscolus, Cocculus, Collinsonia, Coreopsis major, Crotalaria, Croton (fruit), Cypripedium acaule, Cyrilla, Daucus, Delphinium exaltatum, Drosera filiformis, D. intermedia, Echium, Epigaea, Erigeron, Eryngium, Erythrina, Eupatorium coelestinum, E. purpureum, E. rugosum, Euphorbia corollata, Gentiana decora, G. saponaria, Geranium, Habenaria lacera, H. nivea, Hepatica americana, Heterotheca pilosa, Hexastylis shuttleworthii, H. speciosa, Hibiscus moscheutos, H. palustris, Houstonia purpurea, Hybanthus, Hydrocotyle, Hypericum galioides, H. gentianoides, H. stans, Ipomoea sagittata, Jeffersonia, Lachnanthes, Liatris provincialis, L. scariosa, L. squarrosa, Lilium canadense, L. catesbaei, L. superbum, Lippia, Lobelia cardinalis, Lophiola, Ludwigia alternifolia, Lysimachia ciliata, L. quadrifolia, Lythrum, Mimulus, Mitchella, Monarda citriodora, M. didyma, M. fistulosa, M. punctata, Monotropa uniflora, Nuphar, Nymphaea, Oenothera biennis, Orchis, Orobanche, Oxalis grandis, Panax, Penstemon calycosus, P. smallii, Phlox carolina, P. divaricata, P. pilosa, Pinguicula, Podophyllum, Polemonium, Polygala curtissii, P. cymosa, P. lutea, P. nana, Pontederia, Potentilla recta, Prunella, Pycnanthemum, Rhexia alifanus, R. lutea, Rhododendron, Robinia, Rudbeckia laciniata, Ruellia humilis, R. strepens, Sabatia campanulata, S. dodecandra, Sanguinaria, Saponaria, Sarracenia leucophylla, S. oreophila, S. psittacina, S. purpurea, Schoenolirion, Schrankia, Scutellaria, Silene cucubalus, S. stellata, Silphium integrifolium, S. perfoliatum,

Solidago bicolor, S. gigantea, S. graminifolia, Sparganium, Spiranthes cernua, S. odorata, Stellaria, Stenanthium, Streptopus, Talinum, Thalia, Thalictrum polygamum, Trifolium arvense, T. incarnatum, Trilisa, Trillium cernuum, T. recurvatum, T. stamineum, Typha, Uniola, Uvularia grandiflora, Verbascum thapsus, Verbena canadensis, V. rigida, V. stricta, Veronicastrum, Viola hastata, V. palmata, V. rostrata, Warea, Wisteria, Zigadenus

Harriet Wright:
Agave, Allium bivalve, Anagallis, Andrachne, Aristolochia, Aster linariifolius, Cardiospermum, Clematis virginiana, Disporum, Echinacea, Erigenia, Gaura, Gillenia, Habenaria blephariglottis, H. ciliaris, H. flava, Halesia, Heuchera, Hexastylis, Hydrangea, Hymenocallis occidentalis, Hypericum hypericoides, Impatiens, Ipomoea quamoclit, Ludwigia peploides, Malaxis, Melanthium, Modiola, Obolaria, Oenothera speciosa, Osmorhiza, Passiflora lutea, Pedicularis, Penstemon hirsutus, Phacelia, Potentilla canadensis, Sarracenia alata, Seymeria, Sisyrinchium albidum, Smilacina, Stewartia malacodendron, S. ovata, Stillingia, Symplocos, Trichostema, Trillium flexipes, Xanthorhiza, Xyris, Zizia

Mike Hopiak:
Cardamine concatenata, Chamaelirium, Chimaphila, Crinum, Cypripedium calceolus, Delphinium tricorne, Dicentra, Dodecatheon, Eichhornia, Epifagus, Erythronium albidum, E. rostratum, Galax, Goodyera, Habenaria blephariglottis var. integrilabia, Hepatica acutiloba, Hexastylis minor, Houstonia pusilla, Hymenocallis coronaria, Iris cristata, Liatris graminifolia, Lilium michauxii, Liparis, Listera, Lupinus, Medeola, Orontium, Parnassia, Phlox pulchra, Pinguicula caerulea, Polygonatum, Sarracenia flava, Saxifraga, Silene rotundifolia, S. virginica, Spiranthes grayi, Swertia, Thalictrum dioicum, T. thalictroides, Tradescantia hirsuticaulis, Trillium cuneatum, T. decumbens, T. underwoodii, Triphora, Viola papilionacea, V. pedata, V. pubescens

Helen Kittinger:
Aconitum, Aruncus, Asclepias tuberosa, Croton (flower), Dichromena, Eriocaulon, Eupatorium perfoliatum, Hypoxis, Iris verna, Isotria, Kalmia, Monotropa hypopithys, Muscari, Neviusia, Pachysandra, Passiflora, Peltandra, Penstemon

digitalis, Sagittaria, Silene caroliniana, Sisyrinchium angustifolium, Spigelia, Spiranthes ovalis, Tiarella, Trillium catesbaei, T. pusillum, Vernonia, Viola tricolor

Joab Thomas:
Anemone caroliniana, Anisostichus, Asimina, Belamcanda, Calopogon, Carduus, Cliftonia, Dracopis, Helenium, Helianthus, Hexalectris, Houstonia pygmaea, Illicium, Isopyrum, Linaria, Pogonia, Ranunculus, Rhexia virginica, Rhus radicans, R. vernix, Rosa, Verbascum blattaria, Verbena brasiliensis, Veronica, Viola rafinesquii

Rebecca Bray:
Aesculus, Amorpha, Campanula americana, Campsis, Cephalanthus, Cercis, Chionanthus, Commelina, Coreopsis auriculata, C. tinctoria, Gaillardia, Helianthemum, Hypericum myrtifolium, Ipomoea stolonifera, Lamium, Liriodendron, Mertensia, Nelumbo, Saururus, Sonchus, Taraxacum, Zephyranthes

Fairly Chandler:
Aletris, Allium cuthbertii, Aphanostephus, Baptisia leucantha, B. tinctoria, Chaptalia, Coreopsis nudata, Habenaria integra, Heterotheca mariana, Ipomopsis, Liatris tenuifolia, Marshallia, Mikania, Paronychia, Pinguicula pumila, Satureja, Tofieldia, Utricularia

Dolly Stack:
Cardamine, Centrosema, Corydalis, Euphorbia heterophylla, Heliotropium, Hibiscus aculeatus, Ipomoea purpurea, Justicia, Lobelia siphilitica, Sabatia angularis, Specularia, Oxalis violacea, Physalis, Tradescantia virginiana, Uvularia perfoliata

Dock Loyd:
Chrysanthemum, Ipomoea pandurata, Lonicera, Rudbeckia hirta, Tephrosia

Harold Cooley:
Ipomoea pes-caprae, Lycium, Solanum, Solidago arguta

Mary Burks:
Conopholis, Opuntia, Lithospermum

Bob Mills:
Hydrolea, Krigia

Ruth Monasco:
Gelsemium, Gentiana villosa

Bob Cobb:
Claytonia

Fred Fish:
Viola blanda

Louise McSpadden:
Ponthieva

James D. Mason:
Cypripedium reginae

John Scott:
Solidago altissima

LIST OF SPONSORS

Mr. & Mrs. Jack D. McSpadden

William M. Spencer

Birmingham Audubon Society

Alabama Wildflower Society

Mrs. T. Felton Wimberly, Jr.

W. R. J. Dunn, Jr.

Judge and Mrs. James H. Hancock

Mr. & Mrs. Robert R. Reid, Jr.

Mr. & Mrs. Fritz Woehle

Mrs. R. Hugh Daniel

Mr. & Mrs. William C. Ireland

INDEX